Acting Out!

Other Redleaf Press books by Rae Pica

Toddlers Moving & Learning
Preschoolers & Kindergartners Moving & Learning
Early Elementary Children Moving & Learning

Acting Out!

Avoid Behavior Challenges
— with —
Active Learning Games *and* Activities

by Rae Pica

Redleaf Press®
www.redleafpress.org
800-423-8309

Published by Redleaf Press
10 Yorkton Court
St. Paul, MN 55117
www.redleafpress.org

First edition 2019
Senior editor: Heidi Hogg
Managing editor: Douglas Schmitz
Art director: Renee Hammes
Cover design: Jesse Hughes and Renee Hammes
Cover photograph: wavebreakmedia/Shutterstock.com
Interior design: Percolator
Typeset in Cassia
Printed in the United States of America
26 25 24 23 22 21 20 19   1 2 3 4 5 6 7 8

Library of Congress Cataloging-in-Publication Data

Names: Pica, Rae, 1953– author.
Title: Acting out! : avoid behavior challenges with active learning games and activities / by Rae Pica.
Description: First edition. | St. Paul, MN : Redleaf Press, [2020] | Includes bibliographical references and
    index. | Summary: "Current policies in the early childhood field ask teachers to treat children as though
    they exist from the neck up—even though research clearly demonstrates that the mind-body connection
    is vital to development. Rae Pica, founder and director of Rae Pica Keynotes & Consulting and author
    of the Moving and Learning series, advocates for active learning and provides easy-to-implement
    movement activities for child care providers"— Provided by publisher.
Identifiers: LCCN 2019019221 (print) | LCCN 2019980228 (ebook) | ISBN 9781605546964 (pbk. : alk. paper)
    | ISBN 9781605546971 (ebook)
Subjects: LCSH: Active learning. | Behavior disorders in children—Treatment. | Behavior modification.
    | Early childhood education.
Classification: LCC LB1027.23 .P49 2020 (print) | LCC LB1027.23 (ebook) | DDC 371.39/3—dc23
LC record available at https://lccn.loc.gov/2019019221
LC ebook record available at https://lccn.loc.gov/2019980228

Printed on acid-free paper

*To all the early childhood professionals who fight
for the right of children to be children!*

Contents

Acknowledgments

This book couldn't have happened without the encouragement of David Heath, now retired from Redleaf Press, or without the dedication of current Redleafers Heidi Hogg and Meredith Burks. Thanks to editor Christine Zuchora-Walske too, for her loving attention to detail!

As always, I need to thank my "life support": Sheila Chapman, Patti Page, Jody Martin, Kelly O'Meara, and the friends and colleagues I'm honored to have in my life.

Also, I'd be remiss not to mention how grateful I am to the many, many education professionals and parents who have shared their stories with me! Thank you for your trust.

Introduction

Over the course of my nearly four decades in the early childhood field, I've heard a lot of things from a lot of teachers and caregivers. And it saddens me to say that lately I too often hear grumbles from early childhood professionals about how disruptive the children's behavior has become. One teacher of four-year-olds summed it up when she wrote in an email, "I am really at a loss as to how to handle the demanding and disrespectful behavior."

Why are we seeing demanding and disrespectful behavior in children so young? I believe it's due in large part to changes in our education system, a failure of policy makers to understand children and child development, and misinformation parents are receiving about childhood. Let's consider for a moment some of what's taking place:

- Children have almost no time to play—something that early childhood researcher and professor Nancy Carlsson-Paige calls "nature's plan" and "a biological drive" (Pica, accessed 2019c). Experts around the globe agree with this statement.

- We are demanding that children accomplish things for which they are in no way developmentally equipped. We insist that three-year-olds sit still, learn to grasp a pencil properly, or memorize the meaning of words like *hypothesis*, which have absolutely no relevance to their lives—because they have to "get ready for being four." We want them to read by the end of kindergarten, ready or not. All these examples are among the stories I've heard recently.

- Children get little to no downtime, which is detrimental to their mental health. How are they supposed to enjoy their lives when every moment is scheduled for them? Downtime is essential for everybody's mental health.

- We treat children as though they exist only from the neck up and that only their brains matter, when the research shows and good sense validates the importance of the mind-body connection.

- We stifle children's natural creativity and inherent love of learning through worksheets, standardized tests and curricula, and an insistence on conformity and rote—as opposed to active, authentic—learning.

- We pit children against one another with our focus on competition and winning.

- Many children spend hours in front of screens, leading sedentary lives filled with virtual relationships instead of interacting with real people in real life—when the research clearly shows that social-emotional development is critical in early childhood and that in-person interactions are necessary for social-emotional development.

How could these circumstances *not* lead to defiance? Imagine the frustration and helplessness building in children as adults take away their freedom—the freedom to just be children. As they discover they have so little choice. As they become more and more disconnected from the real world and the people in it.

The solution, of course, is to let children be children. That means, among other things, allowing them to experience activity punctuated with periods of inactivity, which is the natural rhythm of childhood. Children need to take part in cooperative activities, which they prefer to competitive ones and which allow them to develop relationships more fully. They need to learn through all their senses, physically experiencing concepts and learning via their preferred method, which is movement. They need to play!

Author Eric Jensen (2000, 38), an educator and researcher specializing in brain-based learning, tells us in his book *Learning with the Body in Mind* that "games support the development of emotional intelligence in children while they facilitate face-to-face interactions, the management of feelings, the expression of verbal and non-verbal requests, the delaying of gratification, the use of self-talk, problem-solving, conflict resolution, and more." When the children in your setting possess these skills, you will undoubtedly have a happier, calmer, and friendlier environment.

I realize that the idea of active children in a learning environment may seem counterintuitive to some teachers. Teachers often worry that they'll lose control of the classroom if they allow children to move about. The children will end up bouncing off the walls, and no learning will ever take place. But the fact is, the opposite is true. When children are forced to sit still—which does not come naturally to them and for which they're not developmentally ready—that's when problems arise.

Just like any other young animal, young children are born to move! When we remove that option, they become restless and frustrated. Restless, frustrated children fidget. They act out. When they're told over and over again to sit still, they begin to feel like failures—at three or four years old—because they can't do what an important adult is asking them to do. When a teacher repeatedly sends home notes with a three-year-old child because he's not able to sit still (true story), what happens to his natural joy? How can he comply when he's not developmentally equipped to do so? How can he see school as a place he wants to be? As a place that's safe? Because he has no choice but to be there, how can he *not* act out?

Even if young children somehow manage to sit still for long periods of time as requested, in doing so they learn more about being compliant than about whatever lesson is being imparted while they sit. We see this particularly in girls (Hanish and Fabes 2014). They learn more about following orders than about the fulfillment derived from exploration, discovery, and independence.

I once heard the late Fritz Bell, the wise man behind Creative Classrooms in New Hampshire, say, "We can keep telling the children, 'Sit still! Sit still!' Or we can accept that they're children and allow them to do what comes naturally to them." If we want engaged children, not submissive children, we have to understand and embrace the nature of children.

As the saying goes, if children aren't learning the way we teach, maybe we should teach the way they learn. There's no doubt that young children learn by doing. By physically experiencing concepts. By being joyful, active participants in their learning.

About This Book

Chapter 1 of *Acting Out!* offers the theory you need to more fully understand the purpose of the activities in chapters 3 through 7. My hope is that when you are acquainted with research about the detriments of sitting, the reasons for fidgeting, the need for active learning, and the link between physical activity and intellectual performance, you will feel empowered and inspired to use the activities in chapters 3 through 7. And you will be able to advocate for them—to explain to any curious administrator or parent exactly why you're doing "this stuff."

In chapter 2, I offer tips for creating a positive learning environment. I've accumulated these tips (many through trial and error) over four decades in the field of early childhood education through working with children, listening to other early childhood professionals, and reading research. I hope that my mistakes and learning experiences will help make your mistakes fewer and your learning experiences more pleasant!

And then we get to the heart of the book: the activities in chapters 3 through 7. Each chapter of activities—"Circle Games for Community Building," "Cooperative Games to Promote Prosocial Skills," "Games That Foster Self-Regulation," "Brain Breaks," and "Relaxation Exercises"—has its own introduction, so I won't go into detail about the reason for these categories here, beyond confirming that I have carefully chosen each to help create the friendliest, most peaceful environment possible in your early childhood setting.

Most of the activities require no materials, but should any be needed, you'll find them listed under the heading "To Have." Under "To Do," you'll find a description of how to conduct the activity or play the game. If there are alternatives (either simpler or more challenging) or extensions for the activity, I've detailed them under "More to Do." Finally, each activity or game includes "Curriculum Connections," a section that lists the ways in which the activity addresses the content areas of art, emergent literacy (language arts), math, music, science, and social studies.

These curriculum connections are essential. While conducting my third staff development training for a county school system, one teacher told me she'd been "dinged" by an administrator for one of the activities I'd shown the group during a previous training. It's my fervent hope that should an administrator, policy maker, or parent ever question why you're doing "this stuff," you'll not only refer to the research in chapter 1 but that you'll also be able to point out the connections between the activity and the content area(s) it addresses. Even better: if you can align what you're doing with local or state standards, you should meet with far less resistance from those who might require you to teach in ways that are developmentally inappropriate.

Obviously, the categories of activities overlap. For example, just because you find an activity grouped with self-regulation games or relaxation exercises, that doesn't mean you can't use it as a brain break. Or you may find that some cooperative games are played in a circle and are categorized as cooperative games rather than circle games because cooperation is their primary focus.

In this book, I propose strategies and activities that allow children to do what comes naturally to them and that also ensure your setting functions smoothly. Because you'll be offering children regular brain breaks, the children will be less likely to grow restless. Because they'll be engaging in circle games for community building and in cooperative activities to build prosocial skills, they will have friendlier feelings toward you and their peers and will be less inclined to behave badly toward others. Because you'll help children learn to relax, they will be calmer. And because you'll help them acquire self-regulation skills in the only way that matters to them—because it's fun!—they will be in control of their emotions and behaviors. All these effects will allow children to fully engage and fall in love with learning, just as they were born to do.

Music educator Émile Jaques-Dalcroze is responsible for one of my favorite sayings. He wrote, "I look upon joy as the most powerful of all mental stimuli" (Jaques-Dalcroze 1931). Your early childhood setting *can* be a joyful place, for both you and the children!

Rationale

What We Know about Sitting

When pediatric occupational therapist Christy Isbell presented a workshop at the annual conference of the National Association for the Education of Young Children (NAEYC) about teaching children who won't sit still, more than two thousand early childhood professionals vied for space in the room. Across the hall, I was presenting a session on movement, and my audience didn't even register in the hundreds.

I found this juxtaposition somewhat amusing. When you're talking about young children who won't sit still, you are pretty much talking about all young children. Isbell wasn't there to tell people how to *make* children sit still, which is what I suspect the audience was expecting; she was explaining why so many young ones *can't* sit still and why it's an unrealistic expectation. Meanwhile, I was offering practical strategies for dealing with this reality.

Sure, we've all seen those old photos of elementary school classrooms from years gone by—the ones with children seated primly in neat rows. Having "control" of the children and requiring them to learn via their eyes, their ears, and the seats of their pants was perceived as the best way to provide an education. And the theory may have been logical back then, when educators didn't have any research to prove there might be a better way. But today we do!

Today we have brain research demonstrating that sitting in a chair increases fatigue because our bodies are designed to move, not sit. Eric Jensen has written extensively about this issue. He confirms that sitting for more than ten minutes at a time reduces our awareness of physical and emotional sensations. Also, the pressure on a person's spinal discs is 30 percent greater while the person is sitting than while the person is standing. None of this contributes to optimal health or learning. Nor does it contribute to optimal behavior. Jensen (2000, 30) writes, "These problems reduce concentration and attention, and ultimately result in discipline problems." So why would we want children to sit more often?

Jensen is just one of many educators and researchers to ring the warning bell about the folly of sitting to learn. As far back as 1929, Alfred North Whitehead (1967, 50), wrote in *The Aims of Education and Other Essays*, "I lay it down as an educational axiom that in teaching you will come to grief as soon as you forget that your pupils have bodies." Recently, an educator told me the same thing in the simplest of terms. He said, "If you don't let them move, you've already lost them."

Despite the brain research now available, today's early childhood classrooms too often still resemble those elementary school classrooms of old, with young children sitting rather than playing and moving. Why do we imagine that sitting equals learning? Why do we insist on pretending that children exist only from the neck up—that the mind and body have absolutely nothing to do with each other? As Isbell said to me in an interview for BAM! Radio Network (the largest education radio network online), "Who's to say we have to sit down to learn? Why can't we stand to learn? Why can't we lay on the floor on our tummies to learn? Why can't we sit in the rocking chair to learn? There are lots of other simple movement strategies. Just changing the position can make a big difference" (Pica, accessed 2019e).

Here's an example of that. In one study, researchers equipped four fourth-grade classrooms with standing desks, and what happened was amazing. Even though the desks were equipped with stools, 70 percent of the kids never used the stools, and the other 30 percent used the stools sometimes but stood the majority of the time. The end result? Increased attention, alertness, engagement, and on-task behavior (Dornhecker et al. 2015). It's a teacher's dream!

Of course, standing desks are expensive, but that doesn't mean you can't allow the children to stand as needed. You could seat children who need to move at the outside of desk clusters so they don't distract others. Or, better still, offer flexible seating, with tables, balance balls, beanbag chairs, rocking chairs, stools, tires, and comfortable rugs, and each day let the children choose the sitting (or sprawling) option that best meets their needs. Because they're being given that responsibility and choice, they will take the decision seriously, and there will be fewer behavioral issues.

Often preschool teachers argue that they must get children used to sitting because the children are going to have to sit in kindergarten and beyond. Unfortunately, it's true that children will have to become accustomed to sitting in school until policy makers begin paying attention to the research and opt for an education system that aligns with how kids learn. But it's also true that kids will eventually have to learn how to drive. Does that mean we should put them behind the wheel while they're still preschoolers?

The solution to the "problem" of children who won't sit still is to allow children to be children. Specifically, adults must first allow them to develop their proprioceptive and vestibular senses. Proprioception is awareness of the location of one's body parts and of one's body in relation to the environment. With a properly developed proprioceptive sense, children are able to perform tasks such as feeding themselves without having to watch their fork travel to their mouth or are able to climb a staircase without looking at their feet. The vestibular sense detects gravity and motion to create an internal sense of balance. It coordinates with the other senses to help a person get upright and stay that way. With a properly developed vestibular sense, children will have, among other things, better balance, visual tracking, and self-regulation. When both the proprioceptive and vestibular senses are developed, sitting is much easier for children.

The critical period for development of these senses is before the age of six. And the best way to promote their development is to allow children to move—to jump, bounce, spin, swing, and hang upside down. Yesterday's children, who had far more unstructured time and access to equipment such as swings and monkey bars, had ample opportunity for these experiences. Today's children, many of whom are enrolled in school and centers from infancy and who are leading highly scheduled lives, are being denied these opportunities. It's no wonder they have trouble sitting still.

What We Know about Fidgeting

When the children are sitting, do you find yourself asking some of them to "please sit still" over and over again? Or, at the very least, are you internally begging them to stop fidgeting?

There's no doubt that fidgeting can be distracting. But too often it's seen as misbehaving. Many a child has been moved down on those awful behavior charts for fidgeting. And some, unable to comply with their teachers' wishes, are made to feel like failures at the ripe old age of three, four, or five. No child should ever feel like a failure. Nor should a child get coded as having attention issues or be labeled as having attention deficit hyperactivity disorder (ADHD), simply because she can't sit still in school—in other words, because she is a child.

While some children may be able to comply with a request to sit still, others simply cannot. In general, children are not suited to sitting still. In fact, the human body functions best when it is able to move.

Pediatric occupational therapist Angela Hanscom is among those experts who contend that children simply don't engage in enough movement anymore, and that's why children are fidgeting more than ever. Lack of movement, she says, has resulted in children having underdeveloped balance systems and strength. She writes, "Children are going to class with bodies that are less prepared to learn than ever before. With sensory systems not quite working right, they are asked to sit and pay attention. Children naturally start fidgeting, in order to get the movement their body so desperately needs and is not getting enough of to 'turn their brain on.' What happens when the children start fidgeting? We ask them to sit still and pay attention; therefore, their brain goes back to 'sleep'" (Hanscom 2014).

Obviously, sleeping brains cannot manage optimal learning or behavior. In a 2008 study, researchers found that children need to move in order to focus during a complicated mental task. Dr. Mark Rapport, the psychology professor who supervised this study, explained that this is why some children have to move while reading or doing math but are able to sit still when watching an appealing movie. Many adults believe that if children are able to sit still during a "preferred" activity such as watching a movie, then they can do it at will. Rapport says this isn't the case; when children are involved in an experience using working memory and cognitive processing, they *need* to move to be able to focus (Bright, accessed 2018).

A 2015 study reported that for children with attention disorders, hyperactive movements like moving and spinning in a chair meant better performance on tasks requiring concentration. Dr. Dustin Sarver, the ADHD researcher who led the study, said that when the kids were moving, they were increasing their alertness and that small physical motions awaken the nervous system in a way that's similar to how the medication Ritalin works (Sarver et al. 2015; Kamenetz 2015). According to Sarver, when we tell children, "'Sit down, don't move, stop tapping, stop bouncing,' the kids are spending all their mental energy concentrating on that rule." And that prevents them from focusing on whatever task we're asking them to do (Kamenetz 2015).

The solution for all children is to ensure that they have more opportunities to move and play in early childhood settings. One way to provide such opportunities is by offering learning centers through which the children rotate and by providing active learning across the curriculum. (More information on active learning follows in the next section.) You'll also find ideas in this book for brain breaks, which invite the children to get up from their seats periodically and get the blood flowing. And recess must take place *at least* once a day for every single child. It should never be skipped for any reason or withheld as punishment. (For more on recess, see pages 24–25 and 87–89.

Here is a list of classroom items for managing fidgeting, recommended by teachers. If you use these, along with the activities in this book, you will have increased attention, alertness, engagement, and on-task behavior:

- bike inner tubes wrapped around the legs of chairs, allowing kids to bounce their legs

- partially inflated beach balls placed on seats, allowing children to wiggle as needed

- chewing gum (Although gum chewing in school is controversial, one teacher told me this was the only solution she could find for a child who was constantly mouthing things. She received permission from the child's parents, and the problem was solved.)

- coloring books (Just because a child is coloring doesn't mean she isn't listening. In fact, this may be her best bet for paying attention.)

- stress balls, koosh balls, and putty for squeezing

- fidget spinners and other fidget toys (used only in the manner and by the ages for which they are intended)

Finally, we need to address the much-loved practice of asking children to sit "crisscross-applesauce" during story or circle time. When children are unable to comply—when they become restless and wiggly—we tend to see it as misbehavior and as a violation of the rules. Instead, we need to examine why such rules exist—rules that run contrary to what we know about children, sitting, and fidgeting. If we understand that children are much more likely to be engaged when they're comfortable, why would we insist that they assume a position that perhaps isn't comfortable at all, often for many long minutes at a time?

Personally, I would feel as though I were losing my mind if someone asked me to sit for more than a single minute cross-legged, with my back straight, and with my hands in my lap. And I suspect a great many adults would feel the same way. So why do we require this of children, who are far more likely than adults to be unable to contain their energy when they're uncomfortable? If we allow children to sit, lie, or stand in whatever way feels good to them, fidgeting will be far less likely to occur. And we'll have engaged and happy children, which should be our goal.

What We Know about the Need for Active Learning

In the past, based on what they knew about and observed in young children, preschool and kindergarten teachers designed their programs to meet children's developmental needs. Play and active learning were considered key tools to accommodate those needs and to facilitate children's education. These were some typical activities in the earliest years:

- sorting and stacking blocks and other manipulatives (providing mathematical knowledge)

- singing and dancing or acting out stories (emergent literacy)

- growing plants from seeds, exploring the outdoor environment, and investigating at sand and water tables (scientific knowledge)

- trying on various roles and interacting with one another at housekeeping and other dramatic-play centers (social studies)

Not only were there fewer behavioral issues in the past than what today's educators are witnessing, but active experiences like those listed above also meant the children were seldom sitting. Movement offered them more opportunity for learning and greater retention than worksheets or listening only can provide. That's because the more senses we use in the learning process, the more information we retain (Willis 2016).

For example, when children are given the chance to physically demonstrate verbs like *stomp, pounce, stalk,* or *slither*—or adjectives such as *smooth, strong, gentle,* or *enormous*—word comprehension is immediate and long-lasting. The same is true when they have the opportunity to move slowly while listening to slow music. In all these instances, the words are alive and in context, as opposed to being a mere collection of letters. Letters are abstract symbols, and young children are not yet ready for abstract thought.

Similarly, if children physically demonstrate high and low positioning and wide and narrow shapes, they develop a much better understanding of these quantitative concepts and the concept of opposites than do children who merely see or hear the words and their definitions. When they act out the lyrics to "Ten in the Bed," they can *see* that ten minus one leaves nine. ("There were ten in the bed, and the little one said, 'Roll over! Roll over!' So they all rolled over, and one fell out!") The same understanding and engagement result when children have personal experience with scientific concepts like gravity, flotation, evaporation, magnetics, balance and stability, and action and reaction. Understanding and engagement lead both to greater academic success and a more positive learning environment.

Active learning also provides valuable experience with body awareness and spatial awareness. This may not seem to be a vital benefit, but it is. When children move over, under, around, through, beside, and near objects and others, they better grasp the meaning of these adverbs, prepositions, and geometry concepts. When they have opportunities to explore direction (forward, backward, left, right), levels (low, high, in the middle), and pathways (straight, curving, zigzag) and to create lowercase *b*s and *d*s with their bodies, they are less likely to struggle with reading and writing.

For several years, physical education specialist Marjorie Corso conducted research on how body-space awareness transfers to paper-space awareness. For example, she found that when children three to eight years old were asked to touch their shoulders, some always touched only one shoulder. Similarly, when asked to jump and touch the ceiling, some reached with only one hand. When Corso requested samples of the children's papers, she found that the quadrant of paper not used in writing and coloring was the same quadrant of body space not used in touching and reaching. For example, if children were always reaching for the ceiling with their left hand, they tended to ignore the upper right quadrant of any paper on which they were writing or coloring (Corso 1993).

Corso's other findings include the following:

- Children unable to cross the body's vertical midline tended to focus on the vertical of the paper, sometimes writing or drawing down the vertical center of the page and sometimes changing the pencil to the other hand at the midpoint of the paper. (Recently, a teacher told me that a child in her class moved from one side of the table to the other in order to write on the other side of the paper.)

- Children who can't cross the midline tend to stop reading at the middle of the page.

- Children who have trouble understanding their personal space often write their letters crowded together.

- Omission of gross-motor instruction may be especially devastating to children who are predominantly kinesthetic learners (essentially all young children).

We use our body awareness and spatial awareness to navigate the world. Not only do they enable us to walk down a crowded sidewalk without bumping into a lamppost or to fit our cars into narrow parking spaces, body and spatial awareness also help us understand the customs that govern social interactions. We learn that we should not be the "close talker" who invades others' personal space. We understand that some people do not want to be touched. When a hug or a handshake is appropriate, we learn how strong and how long it should be.

Body and spatial awareness cannot be learned by sitting at a desk. Like so much else in early childhood, these skills must be physically experienced and practiced if they're to develop fully. When a baby is born, we realize she doesn't come equipped with perfectly functioning proprioceptive or vestibular senses. That's why we play "I've got your nose," "This little piggy," and knee-bouncing, lifting, and spinning games with her. But when she starts navigating her way through the world via crawling and walking, the only consideration we give to her spatial sense is whether she's going to bang into a coffee table. And if she doesn't—or doesn't continually— we take for granted that she'll be able to navigate the world successfully.

Maybe she will. But we've all had children in our classes who line up too closely to one another and who bump into everyone and everything. We've all had children whose desire to "crash and go boom" overrides any respect for personal space. Who hug or tag or squeeze too hard. Who view themselves as clumsy or uncoordinated and therefore lack confidence in their physical abilities. Many a child like this has shown up in second or third grade not knowing her elbow from her shoulder or unable to distinguish the difference between a lowercase *b* and a lowercase *d*.

But there are even more consequences to consider. The research of Roberta Golinkoff and Kathy Hirsh-Pasek has discovered a large gap between the spatial skills of children in lower socioeconomic classes and those in the middle socio-economic classes. The result is that the former struggle with and fall behind in science, technology, engineering, and math (STEM). In fact, this gap, which is already enormous by age three, has a negative impact on a child's math readiness skills at age five. As Hirsh-Pasek told me in an interview for BAM! Radio, "Space and math go together." Only experience with movement can bridge this gap. Golinkoff said during the same interview that children need to physically explore "fancy" words like *over*, *under*, and *through*. Sure, they can learn about them while sitting at a desk. But it is only by physically experiencing these concepts that children will find them meaningful and therefore fully grasp them (Pica, accessed 2019d).

Finally, I must point out again that movement is young children's preferred mode of learning. Surely, if we facilitate their learning in the way that they prefer, we will see more success and fewer behavior problems from the children.

What We Know about the Link between Physical Activity and Learning

Just as there was no brain research back in the day demonstrating that sitting isn't optimal to learning, there was also no research showing any correlation between physical activity (exercise) and learning. Nor was there research disproving the notion that the mind and body are separate entities. If the body wasn't engaged in the learning process, people thought little of it. Teachers were concerned with heads only, and those could be addressed while the children sat. But today the research linking physical activity to learning is overwhelming and just keeps coming.

Still, we have people like one state school board member who, when debating the wisdom of making physical education part of the daily curriculum, said, "If they have daily PE, the kids will be healthy but dumb."

Nothing could be further from the truth. Psychiatry professor John J. Ratey, author of the book *Spark: The Revolutionary New Science of Exercise and the Brain*, calls movement "Miracle-Gro for the brain" (Ratey 2008, 19) and tells us that "what neuroscientists have discovered in the past five years alone paints a riveting picture of the biological relationship between the body, the brain, and the mind" (4).

The truth is, physical activity has been shown to improve mental clarity and focus, improve memory retention, reduce stress, and produce a better attitude toward school! Researchers from the Institute of Medicine (Kohl and Cook 2013) reported that "children who are more active show greater attention, have faster cognitive processing speed, and perform better on standardized academic tests than children who are less active." A number of studies show that children who are physically active actually do better academically than those who are inactive.

Part of the reason for these results is that moderate- to vigorous-intensity physical activity—the kind that increases breathing and gets the heart pumping a little or a lot, respectively—feeds the brain with water, glucose, and oxygen. We wouldn't expect our bodies to function without food, but when we keep children seated, we are depriving the brain of its necessary nutrients and preventing it from performing optimally. When the brain is performing optimally and children are feeling successful as a result, your setting is bound to have a more positive atmosphere.

In the book *Smart Moves: Why Learning Is Not All in Your Head*, neurophysiologist Carla Hannaford writes

> the notion that intellectual activity can somehow exist apart from our bodies is deeply rooted in our culture. It is related to the attitude that the things we do with our bodies, and the bodily functions, emotions and sensations that sustain life, are lower, less distinctly human. This idea is also the basis of a lot of educational theory and practice that make learning harder and less successful than it could be.
>
> Thinking and learning are not all in our head. On the contrary, the body plays an integral part in all our intellectual processes from our earliest movements in utero right through to old age. (Hannaford 2007, 15)

Long before Dr. Hannaford wrote those words, the ancient Greek philosopher Plato contended that perfection could be achieved if education and physical activity were experienced together. He may not have had the research to prove this theory, but Plato was clearly ahead of his time.

Creating a Positive Learning Environment with Children on the Move

There will be times, of course, when you wonder if there isn't an easier way to make a living! The following suggestions, offered in no particular order, won't guarantee you'll never again be tempted to look for a less challenging occupation, but they will help you avoid behavior challenges and create a positive learning environment while you encourage the children to be active participants in their learning.

Implement Commonsense Solutions

Many teachers hesitate to make movement and active learning part of their programs because when they think of children and movement, they immediately form a mental image of children bouncing off the walls. The concept of movement as a method for avoiding behavior challenges feels like an oxymoron.

That's not to say that wall-bouncing isn't a realistic concern. Movement activities can generate a lot of energy. Unless you have some idea of what to expect and how to deal with all that potential energy, the walls could possibly see some action.

Fortunately, all it takes is some common sense to establish a peaceful environment, regardless of how active the children are. One key commonsense solution is using developmentally appropriate practice. Begin where the children are, developmentally speaking. Then build from there with a logical progression of skills. This approach will ensure that the children are challenged but not overwhelmed. Not only can you expect greater success from children asked simply to build on their earlier successes, but you can also expect greater response from them.

Certainly, there are times when kids just being kids can make you feel as though you've lost control of them. But if you *expect* children to act like children, you can get ahead of potential issues and nip them in the bud. If you have realistic expectations, you avoid the frustration that inevitably results from *un*realistic expectations. Here are three typical situations we've all experienced, along with solutions:

- You hand out equipment or props to the children and expect them to stand silently, holding on to the props and awaiting your instructions. But how realistic is that? Young children are playful and inquisitive! If you simply allow them some time to experiment with the props and satisfy their curiosity, they're much more likely to be ready and willing to listen to you and follow your instructions.

- You ask the children to gather around, but some just aren't interested, perhaps because they're in the middle of something they consider more important. If you get started with those who are interested, others will eventually join in. Young children are curious and don't want to feel left out. Their curiosity and desire to belong will win out sooner or later.

- You group the children by twos for a game or activity. Some children object to their partners. Start without them! There's no reason to spend time debating with them—and taking time away from the children who are ready to go—when ignoring the complaining is so much more effective. If you begin without the objectors, chances are very good that they'll stop complaining and join in.

Speaking of taking partners: if you make a game out of it, you'll have a greater success rate. For example, try an activity called Back-to-Back. Ask the children to stand back-to-back with someone else as quickly and quietly as they can. You then count down dramatically from five to zero. By the time you get to zero, the children should all be paired up. Typically, the children will be more concerned with how quickly they can get back-to-back than with whom they're pairing up, because they love games and they love a challenge. But if one of the children complains about his partner, use the solution described above.

Establish Rules

As early childhood educator Darla Ferris Miller (2016) points out in her book *Positive Child Guidance*, "It is more nurturing and less stressful for everyone involved if adults focus on setting the stage for proper behavior, rather than on reprimanding children after they behave improperly." Creating and maintaining a positive learning environment doesn't mean an absence of ground rules. As you know, children need rules and guidelines, and once established, those rules must be practiced and enforced consistently.

You'll want to establish the following two rules to help ensure that movement activities and transitions run smoothly:

- Rule 1: We will respect one another's personal space.

- Rule 2: We will move with as little noise as possible.

Rule 1: We Will Respect One Another's Personal Space

At first this rule may be difficult to enforce, especially with the youngest students, because they often enjoy bumping into each other. So your challenge is to make it a goal for children to avoid colliding or interfering with one another.

You can accomplish this goal by practicing personal space activities, such as bending and stretching or performing other nonlocomotor skills while standing inside a plastic hoop or on a poly spot or carpet square. Invite the children to show you how high, low, and wide they can make their bodies without moving out of the hoop or off their spot or square. Encourage the children to imagine that they are inside their own personal bubble and they're trying not to burst this bubble.

Once the children get the idea of personal space, you'll need to remind them that they always take their personal space with them and they mustn't interfere with anyone else's. Tell the children they are like cars that stay in their own lanes on a highway. One way to get this idea across is to have each child hold a hoop around his waist and practice moving throughout the room or playground without touching anyone else's hoop. If you don't have enough hoops available, the children can hold their arms out to their sides as they move around the room, making sure their hands don't touch anyone else's.

Rule 2: We Will Move with as Little Noise as Possible

Naturally, you can't expect movement to take place in total silence (nor should you want it to). But you shouldn't need to raise your voice or shout to have your challenges, directions, and follow-up questions heard.

If you establish an audible or visual signal to indicate that it's time to stop, look, and listen ("Stop, look at me, and listen for what comes next!"), children will have to be listening or watching for the signal. And if you make the signal their "secret code," they'll actually be excited about listening or watching for it. For a visual signal, you might choose two fingers held in the air or the time-out sign from sports. If you choose an audible signal, your voice may not be the best choice, because the children hear it so often and may tune it out. Also, be sure your audible signal is a fairly quiet one. A whistle, for example, usually isn't suitable, because it can be heard above a great deal of noise—so the children may feel free to be quite noisy.

But to hear two quiet handclaps or finger snaps, the children will have to be moving quietly.

Whatever the signal, it's reasonable to expect the children to stop, look, and listen within two to four seconds of seeing or hearing it. You should have to give the signal only once. This, of course, isn't going to happen the first several times you try it! But with practice, the children will get there.

Employ Divergent Problem Solving

Although active learning must be handled with special care, it does offer you a head start in terms of classroom management. Most important, success-oriented activities aren't likely to inspire behavioral problems, because children experiencing success generally don't *want* to wreak havoc on the class. The same is true of children actively involved and interested.

One technique to ensure successful, active involvement is to use as much divergent problem solving as possible. Divergent problem solving involves multiple responses to a single challenge. This allows children to respond in their own ways, at their own levels. For example, an invitation to demonstrate crooked shapes could result in as many different crooked shapes as there are children in the room. A challenge to balance on two body parts might lead to children with lesser experience standing on their feet, those with more confidence in their stability balancing on their knees, and those with greater experience (perhaps via gymnastics programs) balancing on their hands. An invitation to move across a low balance beam (or a line on the floor) in a forward direction—or to find two ways to do so—can inspire walking, tiptoeing, scooting on bottoms, sliding on tummies, or hopping. (If you ask the children to find two or three ways to do something, be sure there are more than two or three options.)

Here are some other examples of active, divergent problem-solving challenges:

- "Show me how tall (or round, wide, small, and so forth) you can be."

- "Show me how slowly a turtle moves."

- "Show me a kind of jungle animal."

- "Show me a way to move that uses two different body parts."

- "Show me two different ways to stretch (or bend) your body."

Here's an example from the content area of math: challenge the children to use manipulatives to find two different ways to create the concept of nine (for instance, one and eight, four and five, six and three, or three sets of three). Here's an example from the content area of music: ask the children to find three different ways to make a sound with a tambourine (such as shaking it, tapping it, flicking it with a finger, or hitting it with a hand, on a hip, or on the head).

Validate the variety of responses you receive so the children will realize that there are many possibilities, that it's okay to find their own way, and that there's no right or wrong response. This approach will help children become comfortable taking greater creative risks, and they'll be willing and happy participants.

Certainly, many of the activities in this book use a direct approach, in which demonstration-and-imitation is the instructional method. This method is necessary for activities during which you want the children to replicate your movements, such as The Mirror Game or Imitating Movement. However, for activities such as Chair Dancing or Bridges and Tunnels, divergent problem solving is called for because there *are* many different ways to respond. Present the challenges with enthusiastic vocal and facial expression, but don't participate beyond that, because if you do, the children will merely imitate what they see you do. And that won't help promote the children's critical and creative thinking skills or offer them opportunities for enhanced self-esteem.

Use Positive Challenges

If you assume the children are capable of handling your challenges, they are more likely to *be* capable. They will rise to your expectations. For example, a challenge that begins with "Find three ways to…" assumes that the children can find at least three ways to respond. Similarly, a challenge that begins with "Show me you can…" implies that you know the children can do what you ask.

Conversely, if you present challenges by asking, "Can you…," you are implying a choice. Many young children will be happy to say no.

You have in your favor the fact that children love to show off—to display their abilities—especially to you. So if you introduce challenges with phrases like "Let me see you…" or "Show me you can…," children will want to show you they can. This is a simple technique, but it is amazingly effective.

Make Corrections Creatively

Singling out children who have responded incorrectly to a challenge (for example, galloping when the challenge was to jump) causes embarrassment and self-consciousness, and those feelings don't lead to future success. On the other hand, you can't help children learn if you simply ignore their incorrect responses.

The corrective options are to ask children who responded correctly to demonstrate, to describe the differences between galloping and jumping, or to reissue the challenge to give children another chance to succeed. If the same children respond incorrectly, you're alerted to an issue requiring attention. You can offer the attention when it's possible to do so privately and positively.

Use Praise and Positive Reinforcement Wisely

It's okay to praise children—but not constantly. An overabundance of praise can turn children into praise addicts who need more and more every day to maintain their self-esteem. Save praise for deserving accomplishments. Children can sense when adults are being dishonest, and praise will cease to have any meaning for them if it's not sincere.

Perhaps one of the most difficult praise habits to overcome is moralizing. We often say "good girl" or "good boy," which implies that the children are good because they are doing what we asked. Saying "good job" is equally problematic, because it tells children nothing about what was good. For instance, saying "good job" following a child's jump isn't at all informative. But if you describe the jump as high, low, light, or heavy, you provide a description of what you saw and information the child can use.

Many adults have been misinformed that children's need for positive reinforcement means they must praise children for everything they do. But the late Stanley Greenspan, who was a professor and practicing child psychiatrist, said in a BAM! Radio interview, "If you drown your child in praise, then nothing has meaning" (Pica, accessed 2019b). In another interview, psychology professor Ellen Ava Sigler contended that many adults "believe that positive reinforcement is sweets, treats, and empty praise, when positive reinforcement is positive attention. . . . [S]imply acknowledging a child's work or talking to a child about what they're doing *is* positive reinforcement" (Pica, accessed 2019a).

Recognition and encouragement are always going to be better alternatives to false praise and value judgments. When you describe the children's responses with enthusiasm and respect, you validate them and encourage original solutions.

Use Your Voice as a Tool

This is a straightforward and simple suggestion. If you want the children to move slowly, speak slowly. If you want them to move quietly, speak quietly. Also, just as you can catch more flies with honey than with vinegar, you can attract more attention with a lower volume than with a higher one. Children are far more likely to react to a whisper than to a yell.

Although you should present your challenges enthusiastically, if you maintain a fever pitch of enthusiasm, the children will become overstimulated. I witnessed this once when working as a university adjunct. One of my students was conducting a lesson with a group of five-year-olds and spoke to the children at an extremely rapid pace and a high pitch throughout. By the time she asked them to move like turtles, what she got was a group of racing turtles!

Another way you can use your voice as a tool is to say (or sing) the children's names often. A child's name is special. Children love the sound of their names. When an adult uses a child's name in a positive way, the child receives recognition and reassurance.

Monitor Energy Levels

As you well know, movement activities and transitions can generate an abundance of energy. Too much energy can result in frustrating, unproductive, unmanageable experiences. Too little energy, however, can have comparable results. Tired children tend to display irritability and off-task behavior.

Two guidelines offered by the late early childhood educator Clare Cherry are planning movement activities when the children are well rested and not overstimulated from another activity, and discontinuing movement experiences before the children become tired (Cherry 1971). Usually, alternating livelier and quieter activities is enough to prevent frenzy and fatigue. You can also try other contrasts: difficult movements with easier ones, standing activities with sitting ones, big with little, and so forth. Whenever the children have excess energy, channeling it into gross-motor (large-muscle, or big-body) activities will almost always help.

Be Flexible

You need a flexibility of mind and spirit to accept that your ideas will not always go exactly as you've imagined or as you've outlined them on paper (as I foolishly expected when I first began teaching young children). In monitoring children's energy levels, for instance, you may suddenly find it necessary to veer from your original course to either excite or calm the class. Perhaps nothing you planned is interesting to the children on a particular day, forcing you to improvise or go to another activity entirely. Also, young children have wonderful ideas of their own—ideas that would never occur to you.

Be flexible enough to explore the possibilities children present to you sometimes. Not only will this grant them ownership of the activities, but they will also gain greater confidence in their creative abilities. And this approach will most certainly guarantee a happier learning environment.

Don't Insist on Participation

Sometimes, especially at the beginning of the year, you'll have some children who don't want to participate in movement experiences or active learning at all. There can be many reasons for this. Your first task is to find the children's reasons, first by eliminating any physical problems as the cause.

Sadly, some children refuse to take part in such activities out of a fear of looking foolish or being "wrong." Even at a very young age, this fear can be quite powerful. For these children, divergent problem solving and success-oriented movement experiences are the key to unlocking their fear. The children will notice, for example, that eight of their classmates have responded to your challenge in eight different ways, and you're validating each and every response. They'll begin to realize that there is no right or wrong way to respond. With a bit of gentle coaxing and positive reinforcement, you can eventually encourage these children to join in.

Some children are genuinely shy and only need time to get used to the idea of moving with the rest of the group, while others will require specific encouragement from you or another adult. Sometimes merely standing near the shy child as you facilitate movement experiences, offering occasional smiles or gentle touches, is the only encouragement you need to offer. At other times, you may have to physically (but gently) initiate the child's participation by taking his hands in yours and moving them accordingly or by sitting behind the child and rocking him with you to the rhythm of the music.

Positive reinforcement of any level of participation will contribute to the shy child's confidence. For instance, if you've asked the children to freeze and the nonparticipant is sitting particularly still, you can use him as an example of stillness. If you've asked children to move just one body part and the nonparticipant raises an eyebrow, you can acknowledge his response.

At the other extreme is the child who uses nonparticipation as a way to get adult attention. If that's the case, your best bet is to ignore all nonparticipation and offer reinforcement only when the child is involved in group activities.

Whatever the reason for the lack of involvement, nonparticipants shouldn't be forced to join in, as this can place undue emotional strain on them. You can, however, ask that they take on the role of audience. Not only does this involve them to a certain extent, but it also ensures that they're gaining something from the experience, as children can absorb much from observing. Occasionally you may even be pleasantly surprised to learn from a parent that a child who's merely watching in your setting is imitating everything at home.

Create Trouble-Free Transitions

If there were a list of things that young children aren't developmentally ready to do, at the top of that list would be staying still and being quiet. Yet these are the exact two requirements we try to impose on young children during most transitions. We ask them to form an orderly line, to stand still, and to refrain from talking. We then ask them to move from one place to another in that manner, pretending to hold bubbles in their mouths so they'll be silent.

The end result is frustration in both the children and their teachers. And that frustration isn't pretty. During site visits, I've occasionally witnessed teachers resorting to yelling at the little ones to get them to comply (ironic considering that the teachers were shouting at the children for being too loud). It's no wonder transitions come to be dreaded by everyone involved. And it's no wonder that many experts refer to transitions as a waste of learning time. How can learning take place in such circumstances?

But it doesn't have to be this way! Instead of fighting to get kids to move quietly up a flight of stairs, why not challenge them to pretend to climb a mountain? Or, if that still makes too much noise (I happen to believe that sounds are acceptable as long as they don't interfere with the activities of other groups of children), you can invite the children to pretend they're weightless astronauts or cats stalking a bird. Or how about a game of Follow the Leader, with you at the head of the line, tiptoeing in exaggerated fashion up the stairs?

In addition to eliminating chaos (children aren't inclined to wreak havoc when they're engaged), transitions clearly offer learning opportunities. With just a little imagination, you can link transitions to themes and lessons being explored in your setting, adding continuity and the repetition necessary for young children to cement the skills and information acquired. Activities like these also offer chances for problem solving, creativity, and self-expression—and we can't ever have too many of those opportunities. Problem solving, creativity, and self-expression are skills we can be certain tomorrow's adults will need in this rapidly changing world.

Because transitions usually require moving from one place to another, and music is a common partner of movement, movement and music are the perfect tools for transition times. What is more, these are two subjects that today's teachers have trouble finding enough time for. Children love movement and music, and both can change moods for the better. Combining them can turn transitions into pleasurable experiences—even something to look forward to.

Movement activities, songs, and fingerplays provide a focus for the children during transitions, hold the attention of waiting kids, and are easily tied to curriculum content. For example, if you've been studying animals, you can invite the children to move like some of the quietest ones, such as foxes, turtles, or rabbits. If you've been studying the weather, you can ask the children to transition as though they were clouds or a gentle breeze. If you've been studying transportation, the children can sing and act out "The Wheels on the Bus" as they transition.

During successful transitioning, not only will the children learn to bring satisfactory closure to activities but they also will learn to move easily into and out of group situations. Group transitions naturally entail cooperation and consideration, which are important social-emotional skills to develop. In addition, the children will learn to follow directions, which is often the argument made for more stringent transitions.

If we truly understand child development, we know that young children have no motivation to learn something unless it's fun and engaging. If we make following directions fun and engaging, they'll learn to follow directions. And if we handle transitions in imaginative and developmentally appropriate ways—and *plan* transitions, just as we plan other parts of the program—transitions will be trouble-free, tranquil, and filled with important learning experiences.

Don't Underestimate the Power of the Outdoors

When you think about creating and maintaining a positive learning environment, it may not immediately occur to you that allowing the children time outdoors can have a significant impact on their behavior. But it can, and there are many reasons why.

Outdoors, children can engage in large, loud, and boisterous behaviors that would be frowned upon or prohibited indoors. These behaviors allow children to burn off excess energy. Outdoors is also the best place for children to practice and master emerging physical skills and to experience the pure joy of movement. A joyful child is a child who's unlikely to act out. Also, moderate-intensity to vigorous-intensity movement feeds the brain with water, oxygen, and glucose, optimizing its performance.

Getting outdoors is also important because the outdoor light is vital to the immune system, makes us feel happier, and stimulates the pineal gland, the part of the brain that helps regulate the biological clock. Nature experiences have been shown to create a sense of peace in children (Crain 2001) and to generate in children more positive feelings toward one another (Moore 1996). It has even been shown to reduce or eliminate bullying (Malone and Tranter 2003).

Outdoors, the children are more likely to invent games. As they do, they're able to express themselves and learn about the world in their own way. They feel safe and in control, which promotes autonomy, decision making, and organizational skills. Inventing rules for games, as preschoolers like to do, promotes an understanding of why rules are necessary. Although the children are just playing to have fun, they learn communication and other social skills, such as cooperation, taking turns, solving problems, and resolving conflicts.

Finally, after contact with nature, children score higher on tests of concentration and self-discipline (Wells 2000). Children with ADHD are also better able to concentrate after experiences in nature (Taylor, Kuo, and Sullivan 2001). A 2018 study showed that time spent in nature correlates with less hyperactivity and fewer behavioral issues (Sobko, Jia, and Brown 2018).

Many teachers, schools, and districts withhold recess as a form of punishment for any number of infractions. But not only is withholding recess rarely (if ever) a logical consequence for a child's transgression, experimental studies also show that it's the same children who tend to miss all or part of recess day after day, indicating that the threat of missing recess is ineffective. By contrast, recent research indicates that breaks, particularly for young students, are far more likely to improve behavior than withholding recess is (Trambley 2017). Withholding recess is counterproductive for many reasons. If we want to create a positive learning environment, recess must be held—and held outdoors—as often as possible!

Circle Games for Community Building

In early childhood settings, circle times bring about a sense of community—of belonging—that no other group formation offers. Early childhood educator Shelley Butler (2005, 28) wrote that circle times for children have "been around for about a century. Since there is no beginning or end, every individual in a circle is equal and belongs to the whole group." I love that!

Each individual in a circle is significant. Circle time fosters the development of social skills that allow individuals to form a community. Among the social skills fostered "in the round" are recognition of others and both verbal and nonverbal communication. Of course, creating a sense of community is vital to avoiding behavior challenges. To remain part of the circle, children must accept the community's rules and roles.

Whether the children are holding hands or simply sitting or standing side by side, the circle is a symbol of their togetherness. It allows participants to see and hear everyone else. When everyone in the circle moves or sings in synchronization, this enhances the feeling of belonging, even for the child who may be shy or uncomfortable in other group activities.

Twentieth-century American psychologist Abraham Maslow proposed that humans have levels of need that can be understood as a pyramid, called the "hierarchy of needs." Once people have met their lower-level needs, they can meet their higher-level needs. In Maslow's hierarchy, an individual's primary needs are for physical survival and safety. The next level of need is for love and belonging (Martin and Loomis 2007). Love and belonging are especially essential to young children. Because the circle games in this book involve all the children participating (no one is ever eliminated), circles meet the need for belonging. And once this need has been met, children have far less cause to act out.

It's important to note, however, that circle times that require the children to sit in a certain position and simply listen will not necessarily enhance a sense of community. It is active participation by all in the circle that creates community. Butler said, "The most successful circle times include acceptance, openness, and nonjudgmental expression of ideas" (Butler 2005, 28). Those objectives, in addition to the goal of avoiding behavior challenges, are at the heart of the games that follow.

This Is My Friend

This activity is adapted from Terry Orlick's 2006 book *Cooperative Games and Sports: Joyful Activities for Everyone.*

To Have: No materials needed

To Do: Stand in a circle with the children. Everyone holds hands. Raise the hand of the child to your right, saying, "This is my friend, _____." That child says her name, then raises the arm of the next child in the circle, saying, "This is my friend, _____."

The process continues all the way around the circle until every child has had a chance to say her name and all arms are in the air. The group then takes a big bow together.

More to Do: Once the children know one another's names, they can introduce others instead of themselves. For example, Connor might raise the arm of the child to his right and say, "This is my friend, Kisha."

Curriculum Connections: Because this is a cooperative activity, it falls under the content area of *social studies*. Also, the movement occurs sequentially around a circle, and arms are lifted high (a quantitative concept), so it also addresses *math*.

The Name Game

To Have: No materials needed

To Do: Sit in a circle with the children. Clap the syllables of a child's first name while saying the name aloud. For example, you would clap three times while saying, "Sam-u-el." Invite the group to mimic you. Repeat with each child's name until you have said all the names.

Curriculum Connections: Active listening, speaking, and understanding the concept of syllables fall under *emergent literacy*. Rhythm links this activity to *music*.

Name Ball

To Have: A playground ball or small beach ball

To Do: The children stand in a large circle. One child starts by saying her name. Then she gently passes the ball to the child on her right or left. That child says her own name as she catches the ball. The process continues around the circle until all the children have said their names.

More to Do: Once the children know one another's names, you can have them call out the name of the child to whom they're passing the ball.

Curriculum Connections: Because the ball moves sequentially around a circle, this activity is linked to *math*. Speaking is one of the four components of *emergent literacy*. The cooperation involved brings in *social studies*.

Chanting Names

To Have: Rhythm sticks (optional)

To Do: Sit in a circle with the children. Slowly begin to beat your hands (or rhythm sticks) on the floor. Ask the children to join in. Chant your own name four times, fitting your name to the rhythm of the beating. Repeat, going around the circle chanting everyone's name in the same way.

More to Do: Once the children have mastered this activity, you can pick up the tempo by chanting each name only twice.

Curriculum Connections: Rhythm is an essential component of both *music* and *emergent literacy*. (Words have rhythm.)

Say It, Sing It

To Have: No materials needed

To Do: Sit with the children in a circle. Say the first name of the child on one side of you. Repeat that, with everyone joining in. Next, sing that child's first name. The rest of the group then does the same. Follow this by whispering the child's name.

The final step is to simply mouth the child's name, with no sound. Repeat, going around the circle, treating everyone's name in the same way. The children love this!

More to Do: If you'd like, you can add shouting the children's names to the mix.

Curriculum Connections: Using the voice in different ways offers practice in the speaking component of *emergent literacy*. Because singing is part of the experience, the activity also involves *music*.

Bug in the Rug

To Have: Large sheet

To Do: The children sit on the floor around the sheet, spaced so they're not touching one another. All the children close their eyes while you choose one to leave the circle and hide under the sheet. When the children open their eyes, they have to guess who's the "bug in the rug!"

More to Do: To help the children become more familiar with one another, add another challenge. After identifying the bug in the rug, the other children have to tell you one thing about her.

Curriculum Connections: Deductive reasoning is an element of *science*, while the alternate activity offers an opportunity for speaking, a component of *emergent literacy*.

Where's the Clothespin?

To Have: One clothespin

To Do: The children sit in a circle with their eyes closed. You attach the clothespin to the clothing of one child. At your signal, the children open their eyes and look for the clothespin. Once they find it, they put their hands on top of their heads without indicating the location of the clothespin. You then choose one child to point out where the clothespin is. Repeat a few times.

Curriculum Connections: Observation and deductive reasoning are principles in *science*.

Number Ball

To Have: Playground ball or small beach ball

To Do: The children stand in a circle and pass the ball around the circle. The first child counts, "One!" out loud while passing the ball to the next person. The next child says, "Two!" while passing the ball. Continue around the circle, with each child saying the next consecutive number.

Curriculum Connections: The counting and one-to-one correspondence involved qualify this as a *math* activity. The cooperation required in this activity addresses the content area of *social studies*.

Chair Dancing

To Have: A lively piece of music

To Do: The children sit in chairs in a circle. Start the music and invite them to move individual body parts, such as the pointer finger, the hands, the elbows, the knees, or the toes. After they've found one way to move the designated body part, challenge them to find another way to move it.

Curriculum Connections: This is a *music* experience that also offers practice with body-part identification (*science*).

Sew It Up

To Have: No materials needed

To Do: The children stand in a circle with their arms by their sides. You start in the center of the circle and then run in and out of the circle between pairs of children. Every time you run between two children, those children link hands, "sewing up" that hole in the circle. Eventually the whole circle will be holding hands.

Curriculum Connections: The concepts of between, in, out, and in the center fall under the content areas of *math* and *emergent literacy*. You can address *social studies* by holding a discussion about people who sew for a living.

The Spokes of the Wheel

To Have: No materials needed

To Do: Ask the children to stand in a close circle, each child facing someone else's back. The children then extend their arms toward the inside of the circle so all the children's hands are touching. Point out that they have formed a wheel with spokes. The children then move forward, making their wheel spin around and around, while trying to keep all the spokes attached.

Curriculum Connections: The concept of a circle falls under the heading of *math*, while the adverb *around* brings in *emergent literacy*. The cooperative nature of this activity addresses *social studies*. The wheel is one of six simple machines, making this also a *science* experience. To add *music* to the mix, sing, "The spokes of the wheel go 'round and 'round," and so forth.

The Spokes of the Wheel II

To Have: No materials needed

To Do: The children sit in a circle with their legs outstretched in front of them, feet touching in the center of the circle. Their hands should be placed beside their hips. When you begin to sing, "The spokes of the wheel go 'round and 'round," the children lift their bottoms off the floor and scoot one "step" in the same direction (to the right or left). Their feet should maintain contact in the center. Continue this process until the wheel has spun one full circle. (This will take practice and problem solving!)

Curriculum Connections: A circle is a *math* concept, while the adverb *around* falls under *emergent literacy*. The cooperative nature of this activity constitutes *social studies*, the song makes it a *music* experience, and *science* is addressed because the wheel is one of six simple machines.

"Ring-around-the-Rosy"

To Have: Parachute (optional)

To Do: Standing in a circle and holding hands, the children sing the following lines, falling to the floor on the last line. Then they get up and do it again!

> *Ring around the rosy,*
> *A pocket full of posies,*
> *Ashes, ashes,*
> *We all fall down!*

More to Do: Variations include changing the tempo of the song as you go along, beginning very slowly and gradually getting faster, and playing the game around a parachute. For the latter, the children hold the chute with one hand and walk in a circle on the first two lines. While they sing "Ashes, ashes," they stop and wave the chute up and down twice. And, of course, on the last line, they all fall down!

Curriculum Connections: Down and up are *math* concepts. Additionally, singing falls under the content areas of *emergent literacy* and *music*.

Making Music

To Have: One rhythm instrument, such as a tambourine or shaker, for each person

To Do: The children sit in a circle, with you in the center. Make a sound with your instrument. Invite the children to make the same sound. Continue in this manner, making as many different sounds as possible (loud, soft, and in-between).

Curriculum Connections: This is an experience in both *music* and, because it involves active listening, *emergent literacy*.

"The Farmer in the Dell"

This twist on the traditional game offers an opportunity for creativity and more movement!

To Have: No materials needed

To Do: One child stands in the center of a large circle, miming any actions of a farmer that she chooses. (Possibilities include raking, milking a cow, riding a horse, riding a tractor, planting seeds, and so forth.) The rest of the children circle the farmer, singing the following song:

> *The farmer in the dell,*
> *The farmer in the dell,*
> *Hi-ho, the derry-o.*
> *The farmer in the dell.*
> *The farmer takes a partner,*
> *The farmer takes a partner,*
> *Hi-ho, the derry-o.*
> *The farmer takes a partner.*

At the start of the second verse, the farmer points to another child to come into the center of the circle. That child then performs a different farming action while the first child continues with her actions. The game continues with the following verses:

> *The partner takes a child…*
> *The child takes a dog…*
> *The dog takes a cat…*
> *The cat takes a rat…*
> *The rat takes the cheese…*

At this point, all the remaining children come into the circle and together create the shape of a slice or chunk of cheese. Then, ask the children to link hands and sing as they circle:

> *And now our farm's complete,*
> *And now our farm's complete,*
> *Hi-ho, the derry-o,*
> *And now our farm's complete!*

Curriculum Connections: Performing the song brings in *music*, while the exploration of the occupation of farming falls under the heading of *social studies*. Singing is also linked to the speaking component of *emergent literacy*.

Make It Rain

To Have: No materials needed

To Do: The children stand in a circle, one behind another and all facing in the same direction, each placing their hands lightly on the shoulders of the child in front of her. When you tell the children that the rain has begun to fall softly, the children patter their fingertips very gently on the shoulders of the children in front of them while simultaneously tiptoeing around in the circle. Eventually explain that the rain is beginning to fall a bit harder, which means their movements should become a tiny bit more forceful. You can continue this process until there is a thunderstorm. (Be sure the children use their fingertips only and not their hands.)

Curriculum Connections: Rain is an element of weather, which falls under the content area of *science*. Exploring the continuum from light to strong is a *math* experience.

Rotate It

To Have: Parachute

To Do: The children stand around a parachute, facing the center and holding the chute with both hands. Then, remaining in place, they rotate the parachute by passing it to the right or left. Be sure to have them rotate it in both directions.

Once they get the hang of rotating the parachute, they can sing the following song to the tune of "Here We Go 'round the Mulberry Bush" as they do it:

This is the way we move the chute,
Move the chute, move the chute.
This is the way we move the chute.
Here at [name of center or school].

Curriculum Connections: This activity addresses *music* via the singing and *math* via the circle, and it addresses *social studies* by requiring cooperation.

Going Up!

To Have: Parachute

To Do: The children stand around a parachute, facing the center and holding the chute with both hands. Pretending the parachute is an elevator, the children begin with it "at ground level" and then slowly move the chute "up the floors," until it has reached the highest level it can reach. The elevator must then go back down to ground level.

More to Do: You can vary the speed at which the elevator travels and even include stops. How still can the elevator stay while stopped?

Curriculum Connections: The concepts of up and down fall under *math*. Holding still requires self-regulation. Self-regulation and cooperation together address the content area of *social studies*. To bring in more *social studies*, hold a discussion about the kinds of places where elevators are found.

The Igloo

To Have: Parachute

To Do: The children stand around a parachute, facing the center and holding the chute with both hands. For this activity, the children start by holding the parachute close to the floor. Then they raise it, eventually reaching as high into the air as possible, and pull it quickly back down, trapping air under the chute. As simple as this seems, the children will want to do it again and again!

More to Do: To take the game to the next level, you can encourage the children to

- lie down on their tummies as the parachute is lowered, hands under the parachute and bodies on the outside;

- turn to face outward as the parachute is lowered, which crosses their arms and places them inside the "igloo" when the edge of the chute is brought to the floor; or

- let go of the chute when it reaches its highest point.

Curriculum Connections: High and low are *math* concepts, and the cooperation involved falls under *social studies*.

Let It Snow

To Have: Parachute and cotton balls

To Do: Place cotton balls on a parachute. Gather the children around the chute. Encourage the children to lift the parachute carefully. Then invite them to move it up and down in little waves, creating a "snowstorm" and working together to keep all the "snowflakes" from falling off the parachute.

Curriculum Connections: The cooperative nature of this activity qualifies it as *social studies*, while the exploration of weather addresses *science*.

Pass a Word

To Have: No materials needed

To Do: Sit in a circle with the children. Whisper a word into the ear of the child to your right or left. Continuing in the same direction, that child then whispers the same word into the ear of the next child, and so on around the circle. When the word finally returns to you, say aloud whatever you just heard, followed by the word that you whispered into the ear of the first child. If the two words are different, ask the children what they think happened.

Play the game again with a different child starting every round.

Curriculum Connections: Active listening is a component of *emergent literacy*. The cooperative element—and the self-regulation required to wait for a turn—links the game to *social studies*. Moving around a circle sequentially is related to *math*.

Pass a Face

To Have: No materials needed

To Do: Sit with the children in a circle. Begin by making a face at the child to your right or left. Continuing in the same direction, that child then imitates the same face at the next child, and so on around the circle. When the face comes back to you, you make a different face and get it going in the opposite direction.

More to Do: When the children are ready, let them take turns choosing a face to pass around.

Curriculum Connections: Cooperation, self-regulation, and expressing oneself all fall under *social studies*. The sequential movement around a circle links the activity to *math*.

Pass a Movement

To Have: No materials needed

To Do: This game uses the same principle as Pass a Face, but because it involves the whole body, it's a bit more challenging.

Stand in a circle with the children. Perform a simple action, such as jumping one time or bending and straightening the knees. The child to your right or left performs the same action, and so on all the way around the circle. The hope is that the action looks just the same when it gets back to you.

Start again with a new action or, if the children are ready to handle the responsibility, let them take turns beginning the process.

Curriculum Connections: Cooperation and the self-regulation involved in waiting for a turn fall under the content area of *social studies*. The sequential movement around a circle involves *math* concepts.

Pass It On

To Have: One beanbag or small ball

To Do: The object of the game is for the children to pass the beanbag (or ball) from person to person without letting it drop.

Begin with the children standing in a circle. One child holds the beanbag and passes it to the child to her right or left. The process continues until the beanbag has come full circle. Then another child passes the beanbag in the opposite direction.

More to Do: When the children are ready for something more challenging, ask them to pass the beanbag using only the backs of their hands. An even more challenging alternative is for the children to take off their shoes and socks, sit in a circle, and pass the beanbag with their feet. (These variations on the activity should use a bean-bag, as it's less dynamic than a ball.)

Curriculum Connections: The cooperation involved in this circle game falls under the heading of *social studies*. The sequential movement around a circle relates to *math*.

Pass It On II

To Have: One spoon per child and a marble (or another small object that can fit in a spoon)

To Do: This version of Pass It On requires much more concentration and hand-eye coordination. With the children standing in a circle, one child holds the spoon with the marble in it and passes it to the spoon being held by the child to her right or left. The process continues until the marble has come full circle.

More to Do: This game has as many variations as you can think of. In one, the children pass a roll of tape or something else with a hole in the center via either a pencil or a rhythm stick. A simpler variation is to pass an object from cup to cup.

Curriculum Connections: The cooperative nature of this game makes it a *social studies* experience. The sequential movement around a circle brings in *math*. Hand-eye coordination is essential to writing (*emergent literacy*).

Pass a Rhythm

To Have: Rhythm sticks (optional)

To Do: This game is like Pass a Word, except that a rhythmic beat is passed around the circle rather than a word.

Sit in a circle with the children and clap out a simple rhythm (for example, a count of one-two) on your lap or on the floor in front of you. (Counting the beats aloud at first will help the children succeed.) The child next to you repeats that rhythm, and the game continues in a similar manner around the circle.

When it's your turn again, start the game with a different rhythm (for example, a count of one-two-three).

More to Do: Later you might choose to use rhythm sticks rather than hands to add variety to the activity.

Curriculum Connections: The active listening involved in this game falls under the heading of *emergent literacy*, while rhythm is a component of both emergent literacy and *music*. Moving sequentially around a circle links the activity to *math*.

Pass a Laugh

This game uses the same principle as Pass a Face and Pass a Movement, but this time what's being passed is a laugh!

To Have: No materials needed

To Do: Sit or stand in a circle with the children and make a laughing sound. Turn to the child on your right or left, who must then imitate the laughter. The process continues all the way around the circle. You can then go in the other direction, with another child kicking things off.

Curriculum Connections: Sound production falls under the content area of *music*, while active listening is a component of *emergent literacy*.

Over and Under

To Have: A playground ball or small beach ball

To Do: Stand in a close circle with the children, each of you facing someone else's back. Then pass the ball backward over your head to the child behind you. That child does the same, and the ball goes all the way around the circle in this way until it returns to you.

Next, ask everyone to stand with legs apart. Have the children pass the ball under their bodies to the children behind them.

More to Do: When the children are comfortable with both ways of passing the ball, invite them to pass the ball in alternating ways, one child passing it over her head and the next passing it under her body.

Curriculum Connections: *Over*, *under*, and *behind* are prepositions (*emergent literacy*) and positional concepts in geometry (*math*). The sequential movement is also a math concept, while the cooperation involved brings in *social studies*.

How Many Sounds?

To Have: An 8½-by-11-inch piece of paper

To Do: The children sit or stand in a circle. One child holds the piece of paper and begins by making a sound with it, such as tearing, crumpling, folding, or rubbing it. That child counts "one" and passes the paper to the next child in the circle, who must make a different sound and count "two." The goal is for each of the children to make a different sound with the piece of paper, with each child counting consecutively.

Curriculum Connections: How many is a quantitative concept, making this a *math* experience. Also, the production of sound falls under *music*, while active listening is a component of *emergent literacy*.

Doin' the Wave

To Have: No materials needed

To Do: Once the children have formed a circle, ask if they've ever seen spectators do the wave at a sporting event. If necessary, demonstrate the movement or show a video that demonstrates it.

Point to a child to start the wave and then to each successive child to continue it. Once the children have successfully performed the wave going in one direction, invite them to try it in the other direction.

Curriculum Connections: The cooperative nature of this activity places it under *social studies*. It also involves moving sequentially around a circle, which makes it a *math* experience as well.

It's Electric!

To Have: No materials needed

To Do: Tell the children that electricity is energy that flows through a wire. Then stand in a circle with the children, everyone holding hands.

Squeeze the hand of the child next to you, explaining that the squeeze represents electricity flowing from one place to another. Have the child next to you squeeze the hand of the next child, and so forth all the way around the circle. When the "electricity" reaches you again, say, "It's electric!"

Repeat this activity several times, letting the children take turns starting and ending the process.

More to Do: When the children are comfortable with the game, invite them to add an electrical sound effect—*zzzt!*—and a little vibration to their bodies as they squeeze the hand of the next child.

Curriculum Connections: Exploring the concept of electricity links this activity to *science.* The cooperation involved links it to *social studies. Math* concepts are introduced through the sequential movement around a circle.

Every Other

This game is like Pass a Movement, but it focuses on patterning and requires the children to pay even closer attention.

To Have: No materials needed

To Do: Stand with the children in a circle. Perform a simple action, such as clapping twice. The child next to you chooses a *different* action, such as stamping a foot twice. The next child repeats the first action, and the fourth child repeats the second action. The process continues in this manner all the way around the circle. (You may need to offer verbal assistance with this. For example, you could point to Katrina and say, "You repeat what I did." You then point to Nathan, who's next in the circle, and instruct him to repeat what Kia, the child next to you, did.)

Curriculum Connections: The cooperative nature of this activity, along with the self-regulation required, links it to *social studies.* Sequence, a circle, and patterning all fall under the content area of *math.*

"Row, Row, Row Your Boat"

To Have: No materials required

To Do: The children stand in a circle. You designate alternate children to be either A or B. (In other words, the first child is A, the second is B, the third is A, the fourth is B, and so forth.) As the children sing the song "Row, Row, Row Your Boat," those designated as A step forward during the first line (*Row, row, row your boat, gently down the stream*), returning to their places after the word *stream*. The children designated as B then step forward as they sing the second line (*Merrily, merrily, merrily, merrily, life is but a dream*), stepping back after the word *dream*.

This will take some practice, and you may have to orchestrate it at first; but the children will still have fun with it.

Curriculum Connections: Singing makes this a *music* experience. The fact that it involves taking turns places it under *social studies* as well.

"Punchinello"

This game offers a wonderful opportunity for children to reflect on learning experiences, which makes it a perfect wrap-up at the end of the day.

To Have: No materials needed

To Do: The children form a circle, with one child in the center who acts as Punchinello. The children chant the following lines:

> *What can you do, Punchinello, funny fellow?*
> *What can you do, Punchinello, funny you?*

The child in the center chooses a movement skill or other learning experience from that day or week to demonstrate, such as making a geometric shape with the body or performing the actions of a character from a story read aloud. The rest of the children chant the following lines:

> *We can do it too, Punchinello, funny fellow!*
> *We can do it too, Punchinello, funny you!*

Then the children in the circle imitate the actions of the child in the center. If time permits, let every child have a chance to be Punchinello. Another possibility is to assign one or two Punchinellos per day.

Curriculum Connections: Speaking is an element of *emergent literacy*, as is the chant.

Chair Swapping

To Have: One chair for every two children

To Do: Arrange the chairs in a circle, with the backs of the chairs facing inward. Pairs of children sit in a single chair. Designate the direction in which you want the children to move. You then begin to call out a variety of statements. For example, you might say, "Everyone who has a cat (or dog, bird, brother, sister, and so on) at home, move down one chair." Or you might say, "Everyone who has brown (or blond, red, or black) hair, move down two chairs."

This can take some practice to perfect, but the children will find the practice fun—and they'll get some physical activity in the process.

Curriculum Connections: The cooperative nature of this activity places it under the heading of *social studies*, while the counting makes it a *math* activity.

Adding and Subtracting

To Have: No materials needed

To Do: The children sit in a circle on the floor. When you call out a child's name, that child gets up and stands in the center of the circle. Ask the remaining children how many people are in the center. Once they've answered, call out another child's name. That child joins the child already in the center. Ask the remaining children how many people are in the center now.

Continue like this until you've invited as many children as you want into the center, asking the group each time how many there are. Then begin subtracting the children one at a time.

Curriculum Connections: *Math* is the content area experienced here, both with the quantitative concept of how many and the simple computation.

Circle Design

To Have: No materials needed

To Do: The children stand in a circle and place their hands on the shoulders of the children beside them. Point out that the pattern of the circle is uniform (the same) all the way around because all the children are standing in the same way.

Next, help every other child place a foot inside the circle. The pattern has been changed, but it is still uniform. Can the children find other ways they can change the pattern? (For example, every other child can either bend at the knees or stand on tiptoe.) Can the children find an arrangement that isn't uniform? (For example, every child assumes a different pose.) Brainstorm with the children to work out these solutions.

Curriculum Connections: Balance is a *science* concept, and cooperation falls under *social studies*. Creating patterns and recognizing nonpatterns make this a *math* experience.

Cooperative Games to Promote Prosocial Skills

In an essay in the *New York Times*, Nicholas D. Kristof told a surprising story about trying to teach the traditional game of Musical Chairs to a group of five-year-old Japanese children. The surprise was that he couldn't get it to work. The reason? These children kept politely stepping out of the way so their peers could sit in the chairs (Kristof 1998).

To me, this is a clear indicator that competition is taught; it is not human nature, as many claim. The dog-eat-dog behavior becoming more and more prominent among young children in some cultures simply doesn't exist in others. And research showing that competition is human nature doesn't exist; it's simply one of those ideas people have expressed so often that it's become accepted.

Although many persist in believing it's important for children to learn to compete, the truth is that when children are consistently placed in situations where winning is the ultimate goal—where the winners are considered heroes and the losers are considered inferior—winning is what children learn to value. They learn that only the end result (the win) counts, not the process (the effort) involved in getting there. This teaches them that extrinsic reward is more valid than intrinsic reward. Although that may not seem like such a bad thing in a goal-oriented society, we have to remember the young child's stage of development. Children under the age of eight are motivated by pleasure. Winning feels good while everyone around you is offering congratulations, but the kudos don't last and so the good feelings don't either. And what about the children who aren't winning? What motivation do they have to keep trying?

On the other hand, when children are given the chance to cooperate—to work together toward a solution or common goal—the experience feels good for everyone, from beginning to end. Often the children are laughing and giggling. Each child understands he plays an important role in the outcome, and each accepts the responsibility of fulfilling that role. The children also become accepting of others' ideas and can acknowledge the similarities and differences among them. Moreover, cooperative activities rarely cause the feelings of inferiority that can result from the comparisons made during competition. Rather, because cooperative activities lead to more chances for success, they generate more confidence in children.

In *The Second Cooperative Sports and Games Book*, Terry Orlick writes

> the concept behind cooperative games is simple: People play with one another rather than against one another; they play to overcome challenges, not to overcome other people; and they are freed by the very structure of the games to enjoy the play experience itself. . . . Since the games are designed so that cooperation among players is necessary to achieve the objective(s) of the game, children play together for common ends rather than against one another for mutually exclusive ends. In the process, they learn in a fun way how to become more considerate of one another, more aware of how other people are feeling, and more willing to operate in one another's best interests. (Orlick 1982, 4)

Orlick (1982, 22) believes that "cooperation and sharing surface naturally in young children and that the only reason those qualities fade is that they are not nurtured." The games in this chapter are intended to nurture those qualities.

Alfie Kohn's *No Contest: The Case against Competition* is perhaps the quintessential book on this topic. Kohn writes that competition leads to antisocial behaviors, while cooperation fosters prosocial behaviors. He also contends that cooperation

- is more conducive to emotional health;

- leads to friendlier feelings among participants;

- promotes a feeling of being in control of one's life;

- increases self-esteem;

- results in greater sensitivity and trust toward others; and

- increases motivation (Kohn 1992).

There may be times in life when we have to compete. However, if we consider the number of relationships in our lives—familial, spousal, community-related, and professional—we have to admit that there are more opportunities over the course of a lifetime for cooperation and collaboration than for competition. In fact, a survey of employers identifies teamwork ability as the number one skill they want in twenty-something employees (Adams 2013). But this skill must be taught in childhood, just as any other skill is taught. Because today's corporations are seeing so little of this ability, they're spending vast sums of money helping their young employees learn team-building skills.

I hope this information inspires you to include cooperative activities in your early childhood program. In particular, remember that children experiencing success are far less likely to exhibit challenging behaviors and that cooperative games help more children experience success. Additionally, if cooperative activities result in friendlier feelings among participants and greater sensitivity and trust toward one another, that can only be good for the atmosphere and behavior in your setting.

Following are forty-three cooperative games. Some are partner activities, and others are group activities. They all demonstrate to the children how good it feels to be together and work together.

All these activities, due to their cooperative nature, fall under the heading of social studies. Therefore, "Curriculum Connections" will mention only other content areas or the other ways in which the activities address social studies.

Follow the Leader

Although we don't typically think of Follow the Leader as a cooperative game, it *is* a group activity that requires the collaboration of a whole group if it's to be successful.

To Have: No materials needed

To Do: Lead the children around the room or outdoor play area, varying the locomotor skills you use (walking, jogging, tiptoeing, galloping) and the pathways you move along (straight, curving, and zigzagging).

Once the children are comfortable with this game, you can add more variety to your movements, changing their level in space (high, low, midrange), pace (slow, fast, in-between), and force (light, heavy), as well as your body's shape. Also, pause occasionally to perform a nonlocomotor skill (bending, stretching, twisting, and so forth).

More to Do: When the children are ready for the responsibility, you can let them take turns leading.

Curriculum Connections: The ability to physically replicate what the eyes are seeing is necessary for both learning to write (*emergent literacy*) and for *art*.

Monkey See, Monkey Do

To Have: No materials needed

To Do: The children play this game in pairs, standing about twelve inches apart and facing each other. Ask one partner in each pair to perform simple movements in place. Encourage the second child to imitate the partner, like a mirror reflection. At your signal, the children switch roles.

Curriculum Connections: Being able to replicate physically what the eyes see is necessary to both *art* and learning to write (*emergent literacy*). The concept of mirrors falls under the content area of *science*.

Me and My Shadow

This is similar to Follow the Leader, but it is played in pairs.

To Have: No materials needed

To Do: The children play this game in pairs. One child, the shadow, stands behind (and facing the back of) his partner, the leader. The leader performs various movements, both in place and while traveling. The shadow imitates the movements of the leader. After a while, signal the children to switch roles.

More to Do: To make switching roles more interesting (and challenging), as the children are leading and shadowing, occasionally either call out "Switch!" (the children swap places and continue in the same direction) or "Turn!" (the pair swap roles and change direction).

Another option is for you to call out the ways in which the children should move. Possibilities include commands such as "Walk forward," "Walk sideways," "Walk on tiptoe," "Walk while being tiny," and so forth.

Curriculum Connections: The ability to physically replicate what the eyes are seeing is essential to *art* and to learning to write (*emergent literacy*). The concept of shadows falls under the heading of *science*.

Bridges and Tunnels

To Have: Photos of bridges and tunnels (optional)

To Do: Talk to the children about bridges and tunnels. Discuss their shapes, as well as their similarities and differences. Then have the children pair up. One partner forms a bridge or tunnel, which the other child goes over or under. That child then forms a bridge or tunnel that is different from his partner's, and the process continues.

More to Do: Later you can ask trios of children to form two-person bridges and tunnels, which the third child goes over or under. Children take turns in each role, trying to find as many possible solutions to the challenge as they can.

Curriculum Connections: A discussion about the role bridges and tunnels play in transportation adds an element of *social studies* over and above the cooperative aspect. These activities are also an exploration of shape, which is an element of both *art* and *math*.

Seesaw

To Have: No materials needed

To Do: The children pair off and sit facing each other, knees bent and the soles of their feet touching. The children then join hands and rock back and forth, seeing how far they can lower their backs to the floor without touching it.

Curriculum Connections: *Science* is addressed through the cause and effect and leverage involved in this activity.

Bicycle Built for Two

To Have: No materials needed

To Do: Talk with the children about pedaling bikes. Explain the concept of a bicycle built for two. Then group the children in pairs.

Partners sit facing each other. Then they lie on their backs, bend their knees, touch the soles of their feet together, and "pedal." Invite the children to count how many times they can pedal a full turn without breaking contact.

Curriculum Connections: Bicycling is a form of transportation, placing it under the content area of *social studies*. Cause and effect is a *science* concept. Counting is a *math* activity.

Keep It Afloat

To Have: One inflated balloon per pair of children

To Do: Have the children pair off. Give each pair of children a balloon. Challenge them to keep it in the air as long as they can, without either child touching the balloon twice in a row. (In other words, they have to take turns tapping it.) Ask them to count the number of times they tap it.

Curriculum Connections: Flotation and gravity are *science* concepts. Counting is a *math* activity.

Inside the Hoop

To Have: One plastic hoop per pair of children

To Do: Give each pair of children a hoop and invite them both to step inside it, lift it, and move together from one designated spot to another. This may seem simple but can be challenging for the little ones.

Curriculum Connections: Due to the experimentation involved, this can be considered a *science* experience. If you ask the children to count the number of steps they're able to take together, you'll be bringing in *math*.

Matching Shapes

To Have: No materials needed

To Do: The children pair off and determine who is A and who is B. At a signal from you, A moves to a different part of the room and creates a body shape of his choosing. He holds this position until B joins him and, facing him, assumes the same shape (like a mirror image). Once they do this, B moves to a different part of the room and forms a different shape, which A must match.

Curriculum Connections: Shape is a concept falling under the content areas of both *art* and *math*.

Choo Choo

To Have: No materials needed

To Do: Have the children form a "train" behind you, placing their hands on the hips, waist, or shoulders of the person in front of them. Then, calling out, "Choo choo!" the train chugs along, gradually picking up speed. The goal is to stay connected. If one of the "cars" disconnects, that car forms another train with the cars behind him.

Curriculum Connections: Trains fall under the heading of transportation, linking this activity to *social studies*, beyond the concept of cooperation.

Conga

To Have: A piece of lively recorded music

To Do: Start the music and line up the children behind you, single file, placing their hands on the hips of the child in front of them. Start to move around the room to the music, with the goal being for everyone to stay connected in the line. If children do fall out of line, they dance on their own.

Curriculum Connections: Rhythm is a *music* concept but is also part of *emergent literacy*.

Belly Laughs

To Have: No materials needed

To Do: Ask the children to gather together and lie on their backs. Each child places his head on the belly of a nearby child. (Help with this arrangement if necessary.) Point to one child, who says, "Ha!" The child whose head is on the laughing child's belly must then say, "Ha-ha!" The third child says, "Ha-ha-ha!" and so on down the line until each child has contributed a "ha" to the process and everyone is giggling.

Curriculum Connections: The sequential nature of this activity links it to *math*. Speaking and listening are components of *emergent literacy*.

Alphabet Shapes

To Have: The alphabet, posted where all the children can see it

To Do: Divide the children into groups of three and four. Then call out a letter, pointing to where it's posted. The children in each group then work together to form the shape of that letter with their bodies.

Curriculum Connections: Taking on the curving and straight lines of letters and determining the lines' relation to one another prepares children for reading and writing (*emergent literacy*).

Musical Partners

To Have: Music

To Do: The children take partners. When the music starts, the partners move away from each other. When the music stops, they must quickly find each other, hold hands, and sit down until the music starts again.

Start and stop the music randomly. Use varying lengths of time for both the playing and the pausing.

More to Do: This game can also be played in two circles, one inside the other, with the children in the two circles facing one another. When the music starts, the circles move in opposite directions. When it stops, the children hug the person opposite.

Curriculum Connections: This activity gives children experience with *music*. Listening is one of the four components of *emergent literacy*.

Musical Hugs

This is a feel-good game involving touch, which is essential for young children.

To Have: Recorded music

To Do: Play some music and invite the children to move in any way they want while the music plays. When you pause the music, the children hug whoever is closest to them. For the second round, three children should hug. Four children hug in the third round, and so on, until there's just one big group hug!

Curriculum Connections: In addition to experiencing *music*, the children are also using active listening, which is essential to *emergent literacy*.

Bread and Butter

To Have: No materials needed

To Do: Whisper the word *bread* or *butter* into the ear of each child. Try to whisper an equal number of each word. Then give the children a signal to start walking around the room. When they come face-to-face with another player, the two children say their assigned roles. If one says, "Bread," and the other says, "Butter," they hug, fist-bump, or high-five and then go on their way. If both children say the same word, they just move along. The goal is to "butter" as much "bread" as possible before you signal the children to stop.

Curriculum Connections: Matching is a *math* concept. To bring in *science*, before conducting the activity, hold a discussion about the role of bread and butter in nutrition.

Thunder and Lightning

To Have: No materials needed

To Do: Talk to the children about thunder and lightning. Do they know that thunder is the sound that follows lightning?

Children pair off and then decide who will first be "lightning" and who will first be "thunder." (They'll get to be both eventually, so there should be no disputes.)

When you give the signal to start, the pairs separate and move around the room, keeping their eyes on their partners the whole time. When the child acting as lighting "strikes" (moves in the way he thinks lightning moves), "thunder" responds by moving in the way he thinks thunder moves.

After a while, the children switch roles.

Curriculum Connections: Weather is a *science* concept.

Switcheroo

When we ask children to take partners, they naturally choose their best friends first. But all too often, without intending to be cruel, children hurt one another's feelings by refusing to be someone's partner. Because this activity is so much fun, children will be more concerned with how quickly they can find a partner than who their partner is.

To Have: No materials needed

To Do: Designate an area in the room (preferably in the center) to be the "lost and found," and explain to the children that if they can't find a partner quickly enough, they should go to the lost and found. There other children who haven't yet found partners will be waiting to join up with them.

Begin the game with partners standing back-to-back. When you call out the name of a body part (or parts), the children turn to face each other, briefly connect those parts, and immediately return to their back-to-back position. When you call out, "Switcheroo!" children must get back-to-back with a new partner, and the game begins again as you call out more body parts.

Possible body-part connections include the following:

- hands (both, right, or left)
- elbows
- wrists
- big toes
- right or left shoulders
- right or left ankles
- knees
- feet
- thumbs
- pointer (or other) fingers
- right or left hips
- noses (gently!)

Curriculum Connections: Body-part identification falls under the content area of *science*.

Don't Drop the Ball

To Have: One medium-size ball per pair of children

To Do: Have the children form pairs. Invite the children to attempt to move while holding a ball between them without using their hands. The children can balance the ball between their backs, tummies, hips, foreheads, shoulders, or other body parts.

More to Do: Can the children sit down and stand up without losing the ball? (Don't make a big deal out of it if children drop the ball. You want to ensure this is more hysterical than frustrating!)

Curriculum Connections: Both balance and body-part identification are *science* concepts.

Numbers in Motion

To Have: Recorded music

To Do: Play some music. Invite the children to move in any way they wish while the music is playing. When it stops, call out a number, and the children get together with enough children to make up that number, connecting their bodies in some way. When the music begins again, the groups of children move together to the music.

For example, if you call out, "Three!" each child gets together with two other children, linking hands or elbows. Each group of three then moves together until the music stops again and you call out a different number.

Curriculum Connections: The simple computation required in this game makes it a *math* activity. It is also a *music* activity.

It Takes Two

To Have: No materials needed

To Do: Invite pairs of children to match and connect various body parts one set at a time and to find how many different ways they can move without breaking the connection. When they've had enough time to explore the possibilities, challenge them to try another set of body parts. Possible connections include the following:

- one hand
- both hands
- one elbow
- both elbows
- one or both knees
- one foot
- their backs

More to Do: When the children are ready for more of a challenge, suggest non-matching body parts, like a hand to a knee, an elbow to a shoulder, or a wrist to the back.

Curriculum Connections: Body-part identification is a science concept, while how many is a quantitative concept falling under *math*.

Pass It On III

To Have: A beanbag

To Do: Have the children form two lines facing each other, less than a foot apart. Invite them to toss the beanbag back and forth, zigzagging down the lines.

More to Do: Later you can ask the children to find other body parts from which they can pass and receive the beanbag.

Curriculum Connections: The concept of lines—zigzagging and straight—falls under the heading of geometry (*math*).

Cooperative Musical Chairs

In the traditional game of Musical Chairs, at the end of every round, at least one child is eliminated and required to sit against the wall and watch the other children continue to play and have fun. Eliminated children may decide, "I'm a loser," "I'm not fast enough," or "I'm not smart enough." To avoid these feelings, children often resort to antisocial behaviors—poking, pushing, shoving, or tripping—so they can keep playing. By modifying the game to make it a cooperative activity, children learn prosocial behaviors and problem-solving skills, all while having fun.

To Have: Recorded music and one chair per child; one hoop per child (optional)

To Do: Arrange the chairs in a circle, facing outward, with one child standing in front of each chair. When the music starts, the children circle the chairs. When it stops, they sit in the chair closest to them. When the music starts again, you remove one of the chairs. Then, when it stops, the children have to find a way to share the remaining chairs. This continues until there's only one chair left to share.

This challenge has many possible solutions. For example, if each child places one toe on the last remaining chair, the children will have successfully met the challenge! Should the children exhibit unsafe behaviors, such as trying to stand on chairs or piling on top of one another, validate those responses but quickly ask them to find another way.

More to Do: An easier alternative to this game is to use hoops instead of chairs.

Curriculum Connections: This is both a *music* and an *emergent literacy* experience, as listening is one of the four components of language arts.

Buddy Balance

The object of this game is for the children to work together to maintain a steady balance—not to throw one another off-balance.

To Have: No materials needed

To Do: Standing in a circle, the children each place their hands on the shoulders of the children beside them. They then rise onto their tiptoes and count the number of seconds they can remain still.

Curriculum Connections: Balance is a *science* concept, and counting falls under the content area of *math*.

Partner Balance

To Have: No materials needed

To Do: Have the children pair up. Then invite each pair to achieve and maintain a balance that could not be achieved by just one person. For example, one partner provides support while the other stands on one foot. How many possibilities can the children find?

Curriculum Connections: Balance is a *science* concept.

Wide and Narrow

To Have: Wide and narrow strips of paper to use for demonstration purposes

To Do: Using the strips of paper (or, alternatively, a narrow door opening versus a wide one), show the children the difference between wide and narrow. Then ask the children to pair off.

One partner demonstrates a wide shape with his body, and the other demonstrates a narrow shape. Then ask the children to switch roles. Encourage them to try to come up with new shapes and not simply imitate their partners.

More to Do: A more challenging activity is for the pairs to demonstrate wide and wider than. For instance, one child stands with feet and arms somewhat apart, while the second child extends feet and arms to the fullest.

When the children have fully grasped this concept, ask them to form groups of three and to show you wide, wider, and widest.

Curriculum Connections: The quantitative concepts explored in this activity bring it into the realm of *math*.

Balance That Ball

To Have: One large beach ball for every child

To Do: The children form a standing circle, with each child facing someone else's back. Place a beach ball between one child's tummy and the back of the child in front of him. When all the balls are in place, the goal is for the children to begin walking around the circle without dropping any of the balls.

Curriculum Connections: *Math* is addressed as the children move around the circle. Balance is a *science* concept.

Sculpting Statues

To Have: No materials needed

To Do: The children pair off. One acts as the sculptor and the other as the clay. The sculptor gently "molds the clay" (manipulates the child's limbs) to form a statue.

Once all the statues have been sculpted, all the sculptors take a walk through the "gallery," browsing the end results. Partners then reverse roles.

Curriculum Connections: This activity relates to the content area of *art*. However, if you precede or follow it with a discussion about the location and purpose of statues, it can also bring in an additional aspect of *social studies* beyond the cooperation involved.

Hole in One

Parachute games qualify as both circle games and cooperative games but, depending on the challenge, can be slightly more of one than the other.

To Have: A parachute with a hole in the center and a ball smaller than the hole

To Do: Place the ball on the parachute. Everyone then works together to try to get it through the hole in the middle.

Curriculum Connections: Size is a *math* concept.

Light as a Feather

Although the children could be divided into teams that compete to blow the feather off the parachute, a cooperative version offers the children more benefit.

To Have: A parachute and a feather

To Do: For this game, the children sit around a parachute and lift it to chin level. You then place a feather in the center of the parachute and invite the children to work together to blow the feather off the chute.

Curriculum Connections: Lightness is a quantitative concept, which places this activity under the content area of *math*. Cause and effect (causing the feather to move with the breath) is *science*, as is any discussion or exploration of the lungs' functions.

Time's Up

To Have: A parachute and a few small balls

To Do: Gather the children around the parachute and place the balls on top of it. Explain that the challenge is to lift the parachute and make ripples with it (moving it lightly up and down) while keeping the balls from falling off.

Set the timer. At your signal, the children begin, counting the number of times they lift the parachute. When the time is up (allow perhaps thirty seconds to begin with), the children tell you how many times they were able to lift the parachute without losing any of the balls. (If any balls fall before the timer goes off, reset the timer and start again.)

Each time you play this game, set the timer for a little longer.

More to Do: An alternate game is to reverse the goal: time the children to see how quickly they can shake all the balls off the parachute. With this variation, you probably want to use more than a few balls.

Curriculum Connections: *Science* is experienced here through the concept of cause and effect. The concept of time and counting falls under *math*.

Sticky Popcorn

To Have: No materials needed

To Do: Talk to the children about the process of cooking popcorn—from cold kernels through heating to bursting into fluffy popcorn. What would happen if something sticky, like honey or caramel, were poured all over the popcorn?

Invite the children to get on the floor, in the smallest shapes possible, imagining they're tiny, cold, uncooked kernels of popcorn. Then they start to heat up, and they start popping. The "kernels" keep popping all over the room!

Now tell them you're going to "pour" honey or caramel all over them, making them very sticky. When that happens, every time they come near another kernel, they stick to it until there's just one big, sticky popcorn ball.

Curriculum Connections: Nutrition (food) falls under the content area of *science*, as does exploration of the process of heated kernels expanding and popping.

Blob Tag

To Have: No materials needed

To Do: Choose one child to be it. Play tag. Everybody tagged then also becomes it and must stay close to the original it. The result is a cluster of children that keeps growing until there's just one big it blob running around together.

The last person tagged is the first person to be it in the next round.

Curriculum Connections: To make *math* part of this activity, have the children count consecutively as each child is tagged.

Tail of the Snake

To Have: No materials needed

To Do: The children line up single file, each with hands on either the shoulders or the hips of the child in front of him. At your signal, the player at the front of the line (the head of the snake) tries to tag the player at the end of the line (the snake's tail)—without the snake coming apart.

If the snake does come apart, the children should try to put it back together again quickly. If the player in front manages to catch the snake's tail, he goes to the end of the line and becomes the tail for the next round.

Curriculum Connections: Consideration of snakes falls under the content area of *science*. Discussing snakes before beginning the game can reinforce the lesson.

Matching Numbers

To Have: Two sets of ten cards marked with the numbers 0 through 9

To Do: Give one card to each child, who holds it at chest level facing outward. At your signal, the children begin walking around the room in search of a card that matches the one they're holding. Once children pair up, they continue walking side by side until all the numbers are paired.

When the children are all in pairs, you can organize a number parade by putting the pairs in sequential order and having the children march around the room holding their cards in the air.

Curriculum Connections: Because this activity involves number recognition and sequencing, it is clearly a *math* experience.

Three-Legged Creatures

To Have: One long scarf per pair of children

To Do: Have the children pair up, and ask the partners to stand side by side. Then gently tie the inside legs of each pair together with the scarf. Now challenge the partners to count how many steps they can take in a predetermined amount of time.

More to Do: More challenging is finding other locomotor skills they can perform as three-legged creatures. Possibilities include jumping (in this case, on three feet), hopping (on two feet, lifting either the inside or the outside legs), and galloping (with either the inside or the outside feet leading). If the children are able to skip on both sides of the body and with the correct rhythm, you can add skipping to the list.

Curriculum Connections: How many is a quantitative concept falling under the content area of *math*, as are counting and the concept of time.

The Snake

To Have: No materials needed

To Do: Talk to the children about snakes and other creatures, like eels and worms, that move along the ground without legs. Explain that this type of movement is called slithering.

To begin, the children pair off and then stretch out on their bellies, one in front of the other. The child in back takes hold of the ankles of the child in front, forming a two-person "snake." The children then see how far they can slither without breaking apart.

More to Do: A more challenging alternative, once the children have mastered slithering in pairs, is for the two-person snakes to connect with other two-person snakes and to keep slithering. Eventually the children should form one big snake.

Curriculum Connections: Consideration of snakes, eels, worms, and other creatures makes this a *science* activity. If the children count by twos in the alternate activity, they'll be doing *math*.

Palm to Palm

To Have: No materials needed

To Do: Have the children pair off, and ask the partners to stand facing each other with their arms extended and palms touching. They then drop their arms to their sides, close their eyes, turn around in a complete circle, and try to once again touch palms with their eyes closed.

More to Do: Once the children have mastered this, challenge pairs to turn around more than once before reconnecting.

Curriculum Connections: If you introduce this activity with a discussion of what it's like to be a person with vision challenges, you'll be bringing a different aspect of *social studies* into it. Once and more than once are quantitative concepts (*math*).

Up We Go!

To Have: No materials needed

To Do: Have the children pair up. Partners sit back-to-back, with their elbows linked, and try to stand up. If they succeed, encourage them to try to sit back down while their elbows are still linked.

Curriculum Connections: The concepts of up and down are positional concepts falling under the content area of *math*. The balance required is a component of *science*.

Build a Story

To Have: No materials needed

To Do: Sit with the children in a circle and begin telling a story with a line such as, "Once upon a time, a little girl and boy...."

Invite the child to your right or left to continue the story from there, contributing no more than two sentences. Continue the process all the way around the circle, with each child adding to the story. Encourage the children to conclude the story by the time all of them have had a turn. If the story doesn't have what the children feel is a satisfactory ending, supply one yourself!

Curriculum Connections: Speaking is one of the four components of language arts, making this an *emergent literacy* activity. This activity may even inspire a love of stories and reading. Since the story is created sequentially around a circle, *math* is also involved.

Footsie Rolls

This activity may be challenging, but even if the children can't quite manage it, they'll have fun trying. Because the activity requires enough space to move safely, you may need to limit the number of participants to one pair at a time. Invite the remaining children to act as the audience, cheering on the active pair.

To Have: Plenty of space

To Do: Have the children form pairs. Partners lie on their backs, with the soles of their feet touching. They then try to roll across the floor without their feet breaking contact. Should they master this going in one direction, they should try it in the other direction.

Curriculum Connections: The identification of body parts, such as the soles of the feet, constitutes *science*, as does the momentum the children create with their rolling.

Ducks, Cows, Cats, and Dogs

To Have: No materials needed

To Do: With the children seated and scattered throughout the room, whisper the name of one of the animals—duck, cow, cat, dog—in each player's ear. Once each child has been assigned an animal, ask the children to get on their hands and knees and close their eyes. When you give the signal to start, they begin moving around the room with their eyes still closed, making the sound of their animal and trying to find the other animals like them.

Let the children know when all the animals of one type (the cats, for example) have found one another. These children can then sit and watch the others who are still searching for their group members. When all the animals have found their groups, ask the children to count the number of animals in their group.

More to Do: If you're playing with younger, less experienced children, you can reduce the number of animals. If you're playing with older children—or children who've played the original version many times—you can add other animals to the mix, as long as they're animals with distinct and familiar sounds. Possibilities include chickens, pigs, or sheep.

Curriculum Connections: Considering animals constitutes *science*, while sound production falls under *music* and listening under *emergent literacy*. If you count the number of animals that end up in each group, you'll have added *math* to the experience. You can also follow up by asking the children to draw their animals, adding *art* to the mix.

The Machine

To Have: No materials needed

To Do: Choose one child to begin. That child performs a movement that can be done while remaining in one spot and can be performed repeatedly without tiring. (An example would be raising and lowering an arm.) A second child joins in, standing near the first and contributing a different movement that relates in some way to the first. (For example, if the first child is raising and lowering an arm, the second child might move his arm underneath the first child's raised arm and then pull it back.)

One after another, the children join in, each contributing a functioning part to the "machine," which can take on any shape, growing in different directions. Once the machine is fully formed, each part makes a sound that represents its movement.

Curriculum Connections: Machinery falls under the content area of *science*, while sound production belongs under the heading of *music*.

Games That Foster Self-Regulation

Teachers are facing an increasing number of behavioral issues, and we understand that children develop the foundation for self-regulation in the first five years of life. So fostering self-regulation has become an important goal for today's early childhood professionals. Still, there's some confusion about what self-regulation is and how it should be promoted.

Many believe self-regulation is all about self-control. Self-control is indeed a factor, but self-regulation specifically refers to the ability to regulate oneself without intervention from an outside source, such as another person. Self-regulation in young children means that adults don't always have to be telling the children how to behave. They've learned to control their emotions and resist impulsive behavior on their own.

The ability to regulate oneself is something we want for every individual. But many adults are going about teaching self-regulation in the wrong way. Adults often insist that children "sit still" or "be quiet," and they assume that once children meet these unrealistic expectations, they have acquired the ability to self-regulate. Not only does this fail to meet a key requirement of self-regulation (no outside intervention) but such demands typically are also met with resistance in the form of behavioral issues. Young children simply aren't developmentally ready to sit still or stay quiet.

So how do we go about fostering self-regulation in young children? This might surprise you, but one of the best ways for children to learn to regulate themselves is through movement games! As with any skill, if learning self-regulation is fun for children, they feel much more inclined to do it.

For example, if you ask children to keep still, it's not likely to happen. However, if you're playing a game of Statues, which challenges children to move while the music is playing and freeze into "statues" when the music is paused, children will *want* to stay still—because pretending to be a statue is fun. Similarly, *telling* children to move slowly won't inspire them to learn how. Moving slowly requires a great deal more self-control than moving quickly. But asking children to move like astronauts floating in outer space or as though they're trying to walk through peanut butter provides a fun incentive for them to move slowly. And therefore they learn how. The same principle applies to waiting. Waiting is not a young child's strong suit. But if you give children a good reason to wait, as with Blast Off, the first activity in this chapter, they're happy to do it.

Lori G. Skibbe, associate professor in the Department of Human Development and Family Studies at Michigan State University, and her fellow researchers followed a group of children from preschool to second grade and used the game Simon Says (also in this chapter) to assess the children's ability to self-regulate. They discovered that the earlier children acquired their self-regulation skills, the faster the skills developed. Their study also found that the benefits of self-regulation don't dwindle over time. Moreover, the study demonstrated that the ability to self-regulate not only improves behavior in young children but also improves their language and literacy development (Skibbe et al. 2019).

The games and activities that follow are all intended to help children have fun while learning and mastering self-regulation skills. Because self-regulation falls under the content area of social studies, "Curriculum Connections" for these activities mention social studies only if the activities address social studies in additional ways.

Blast Off

To Have: No materials needed

To Do: The children squat low, pretending to be rockets on their launchpads. You then count backward dramatically from ten to one. When you say, "Blast off!" the children launch themselves upward. Repeat as long as the children stay interested.

Curriculum Connections: Learning about rockets places this activity under the heading of *science*. Counting backward, of course, is a *math* activity.

Statues

To Have: A piece of recorded music that lends itself to movement

To Do: Start playing the music. Invite the children to move while the music is playing and to freeze into a statue when the music stops. They're to remain like statues until the music starts again.

Stop and start the music at random intervals. Surprise the children by varying the amount of time during which you play and pause the music.

Curriculum Connections: In addition to experiencing elements of *music*, the children are exposed to a *science* concept if you discuss the muscle tension involved in holding oneself still. You can also make *social studies* a part of the activity by discussing what kind of statues the children have seen and where they've seen them.

Hold That Statue

To Have: A piece of recorded music that lends itself to movement

To Do: Play this game as you would play regular Statues, but in this version, when the children are freezing like statues, you count aloud the number of seconds they're frozen. Vary the counts during which you pause the music.

Curriculum Connections: This is a *music* experience. You can also make *social studies* a part of the activity by discussing what kind of statues the children have seen and where they've seen them. Also, the counting brings in *math*.

Simon Says

In the traditional game, those children who need the most practice with listening skills, body-part identification, concentration, or self-control are often the first to be eliminated. You can promote development of these skills in all the children by playing this game without the elimination process.

To Have: No materials needed

To Do: Organize the children into two groups (two lines or two circles). Explain that the children should do as you say only when the command begins with the words *Simon says*. Then, issue commands like the ones below, sometimes beginning with *Simon says* and sometimes not:

- Raise your arms.
- Touch your toes.
- Wiggle your nose.
- Bend and touch your knees.
- Make a funny face.
- Touch your head.
- Touch your shoulders.
- Stand on one foot.

- Blink your eyes.
- Stand up tall.
- Pucker your lips.

- Put your hands on your hips.
- Reach for the sky.
- Give yourself a hug!

Curriculum Connections: Body-part identification falls under the content area of *science*, while listening skills are significant to *emergent literacy*.

Traffic Lights

To Have: Three large pieces of paper: one green, one yellow, and one red

To Do: Hold up the green paper and invite the children to walk around the room or outdoor area, pretending that they're driving cars. When you hold up the yellow paper, the children walk in place. When you hold up the red paper, the children come to a complete stop. Only the green paper can get them "driving" around again.

Curriculum Connections: The concept of traffic lights falls under the heading of transportation, which is part of *social studies*. Color is an element of *art*.

Red Light, Green Light

In the traditional version of this game, children who fail to stop when they're supposed to are sent back to the starting line. There's also just one winner, with the rest of the children losing. With a slight modification, the game involves more physical activity, more learning concepts, and more fun for everyone!

To Have: No materials needed

To Do: Ask the children to line up side by side at a designated starting line. Acting as the "stoplight," stand at a distance from the children with your back to them. You alternately call out "Green light!" (keeping your back to the children) to signal the children to move forward or "Red light!" (turning quickly to face the children) to make them stop.

When you say, "Green light!" the children run or tiptoe toward you. When you say, "Red light!" everyone must stop and hold very still. If you see players who haven't been able to stop quickly enough and are still moving forward, designate them to be at a yellow light, which means they must walk in place until you give the signal to go again.

When someone finally reaches the stoplight, the game starts all over again. This time someone else acts as the stoplight.

Curriculum Connections: The concept of traffic lights falls under the heading of transportation, which is part of *social studies*.

Directing Traffic

To Have: No materials needed

To Do: Tell the children you are going to pretend that you are a police officer directing traffic, and they will be the traffic. Show and explain to the children the hand signals you will use to tell them to move forward, move backward, move right ("to this side"), move left ("to that side"), and walk in place. Then direct the children as though you are directing traffic, using hand signals only.

Curriculum Connections: Direction is a component of *art* and of reading and writing (*emergent literacy*). Exploring the actions of a police officer directing traffic brings in an additional component of *social studies*, above and beyond self-regulation.

Do as I Say

To Have: No materials required

To Do: Tell the children that you're going to call out different commands for them to follow, one at a time. Possible commands include *walk, stop, jump, turn, stretch, bend, march, tiptoe,* and so forth. You can repeat each command as often as you like, even using the same command multiple times consecutively.

More to Do: When the children are ready, call out two or three commands together, such as *walk-stop, stretch-turn,* or *walk-stop-stretch.*

Curriculum Connections: Active listening is an essential component of *emergent literacy*.

Do as I Do

To Have: No materials needed

To Do: This game is similar to both Do as I Say and The Mirror Game. Instead of calling out commands, as in Do as I Say, simply perform movements throughout the room that the children will also have to do. For example, if you begin walking, the children begin walking. When you stop, they stop. If you jump, they jump.

Curriculum Connections: Being able to physically replicate what the eyes see is essential to learning to write (*emergent literacy*) and to creating *art*.

Zig and Zag

To Have: No materials needed

To Do: The children begin scattered around the room or outdoor play area. When you call out, "Go!" they begin to run around. When you call out, "Zig!" they move quickly to the right (or in one designated direction). When you call out, "Zag!" they move quickly to the left (or in the other direction). Eventually you can begin calling out the directions faster and faster. The faster you go, the more self-regulation will be required.

Curriculum Connections: Active listening is a component of *emergent literacy*. Because the children will have to cooperate to share the space successfully, this adds another element of *social studies* to that of self-regulation.

Step Forward

To Have: The numbers 1 to 10 written on individual cards

To Do: Ask the children to line up side by side at one end of the room. Stand facing them at the opposite end of the room and hold up one of the cards for them to see. (Start with a low number.) The children then take that number of steps toward you, counting aloud as they walk. You then hold up a different card to continue the game.

More to Do: When you repeat this activity, you can give the children the opportunity to practice other locomotor skills, replacing the steps with jumps, hops, gallops, or leaps.

Curriculum Connections: This activity promotes number recognition, counting, and one-to-one correspondence, making it a *math* experience.

Moving Fast, Moving Slowly

Alternating between fast and slow movement promotes self-regulation and helps children fully realize the contrast between the two.

To Have: No materials needed

To Do: Invite the children to pretend to be the following animals and objects, alternating between the two lists:

Fast	*Slow*
a fire engine	a turtle
a jet plane	the hands of a clock
an arrow	a snail
the wind	a train just starting up
a cheetah	the sun rising
a spaceship	a snowman melting

Curriculum Connections: Time and speed are *math* concepts. Allowing the children to express themselves falls under the content area of *social studies*.

Slow Going

Want children to learn to move slowly? Give them a reason to move slowly!

To Have: No materials needed

To Do: Invite the children to pretend the following scenarios or anything else you can think of that brings slowness to mind:

- a cat stalking a bird
- a person walking through peanut butter
- a person walking through deep snow or mud
- a turtle

- a snail
- a sloth
- a car with flat tires
- an astronaut floating in outer space

Curriculum Connections: The concepts of time and speed fall under the content area of *math*. Self-expression is a *social studies* concept.

Getting Fast, Getting Slow

To Have: No materials needed

To Do: This game is similar to Follow the Leader, except that you walk very slowly and gradually increase your tempo. Once you're going as fast as you want to be going, gradually decrease your tempo.

Curriculum Connections: Gradually increasing tempo (accelerando) and gradually decreasing tempo (ritardando) are elements of *music*. Walking slowly and quickly gives children experience with adverbs (*emergent literacy*).

Being Seeds

This activity offers yet another opportunity for the children to move slowly and to use their imagination.

To Have: No materials needed

To Do: Talk to the children about how seeds are planted in the ground and how, with rain and sunshine, the seeds slowly grow into flowers, vegetables, trees, or other plants. Ask the children what they would like to grow into if they were seeds.

Once the children have made their decisions, invite them to get on the floor in the smallest possible shape, imagining that they're tiny seeds planted in the earth. Move around the room, alternately pretending to be sunshine and rain, and encouraging the children to grow *very slowly* until they're as big as they can be, taking on the shapes of whatever plants they've chosen.

Curriculum Connections: The concept of growing seeds is, of course, *science*. You might choose to do this activity when you're planting actual seeds in your setting or in your outdoor area. The word *slowly* is an adverb, which falls under the content area of *emergent literacy*.

Fast and Slow Words

To Have: Slow and fast movement words, posted where the children can see them. Slow movement words might be *stomp*, *trudge*, *meander*, and *sneak*. Fast possibilities include *hurry*, *fly*, *run*, *dash*, and *scurry*.

To Do: Talk to the children about the meaning of each of these words. Then invite them to demonstrate the words as you call them out, alternating between the slow ones and the fast ones.

Curriculum Connections: Word comprehension is essential to *emergent literacy*.

Instant Replay

Imitating instant replay is a fun way to encourage children to move slowly.

To Have: No materials needed

To Do: Ask the children if they've ever seen instant replay on television—for instance, during a sports game or a race. Talk with the children about the fact that an instant replay is shown in slow motion, which is *much* slower than real-life movement. Then invite them to move as though they are in a slow-motion instant replay. If the children like, they can act out an entire scene.

Curriculum Connections: If you talk about some of the professions of people sometimes shown in instant replay, you can link this activity to *social studies*. Time and speed are *math* concepts.

The Tightrope

To Have: One or more long ropes or masking tape (optional)

To Do: If you have ropes, lay them on the floor in straight lines. If you're using masking tape, apply several lengths of it to the floor. Having more than one "tightrope" will reduce waiting time. (If you don't have ropes or tape, the children can use an existing line on the flooring or carpet or simply imagine they're walking a tightrope.)

Talk to the children about what tightrope walkers do and where they work. Discuss the balance and control this profession requires. Then invite the children to take turns walking the length of the rope.

More to Do: Later you can ask the children to show you what other locomotor skills they might use to travel across the tightrope. You can also invite them to try moving sideways and eventually backward on a tightrope. (The latter takes a *lot* of control!)

Curriculum Connections: Exploring the occupation of circus performers constitutes *social studies*, while balance is a *science* concept.

Turn, Turn, Turn

To Have: Ropes or lines laid or drawn on the floor

To Do: Invite the children to move from one end of the "tightrope" to the other while making slow turns in one direction. They then return to the original starting point by turning in the other direction.

Curriculum Connections: Balance is a *science* concept. If you include a discussion about circus performers, that will add another element of *social studies*.

Let's Focus

This activity requires the children to isolate head movement and to use their imagination to the maximum in order to vary their responses.

To Have: No materials needed

To Do: Invite the children to focus their gaze as if they are doing the following:

- searching for something small on a rug
- looking out a car window
- trying to see in a dark room
- watching a falling star
- watching a parade

- being hypnotized by a swinging object
- looking through a telescope
- looking through a microscope
- watching a tennis game
- looking at an airplane

Curriculum Connections: By focusing on the sense of sight, this activity qualifies as a *science* experience.

Blind Movement

To Have: No materials needed

To Do: Ask the children to perform the following movements with their eyes closed:

- touching a pointer finger to the tip of the nose
- standing on tiptoe
- standing flat on one foot

- leaning forward (or backward, to one side, to the other side)
- swaying

Curriculum Connections: Focusing on the sense of sight, or lack thereof, places this activity under the heading of *science*. Any discussion of individuals with visual challenges would fall under *social studies*.

Body-Part Boogie

This game is similar to Statues, but it's more challenging because it requires the children to isolate individual body parts. Even if children can't isolate and move the designated body part, they'll still have fun trying.

To Have: A piece of recorded music that lends itself to movement

To Do: Ask the children to stand in a circle or have them scatter throughout the room. Tell them they must stand completely still, like statues.

Play a piece of music and designate just one body part for the children to move to the music (for example, the head, an arm, a foot, a leg, fingers). When you pause the music, they must freeze again.

More to Do: If you use different styles of music every time you play this game, you'll inspire different kinds of movement.

Curriculum Connections: In addition to experience with the content area of *music*, this activity requires active listening, which is part of *emergent literacy*. Also, body-part identification falls under the heading of *science*.

Sleeping Giants

Children love this simple game.

To Have: No materials needed

To Do: Invite the children to jump up and down until you call out, "Sleeping giants!" They then collapse to the floor and lie very still. When you call out, "Waking giants!" the children start jumping again.

Curriculum Connections: If you talk with the children about sleeping and waking, you can connect this activity to *science*. If you read a story about giants, you can connect it to *emergent literacy*.

Beanbag Freeze

To Have: One beanbag per child

To Do: After you've handed out the beanbags, explain that the children are to walk around the room with their beanbags balanced on a specific body part, which you'll designate. If the beanbag falls, the player has to freeze in that spot and wait until another player has retrieved the beanbag for her. If the second player's beanbag also falls, that player freezes too, until help comes along. Begin by challenging the children to balance their beanbags on simple body parts, such as their palm or the back of a hand.

More to Do: Later, when the children are ready, you can invite them to carry their beanbags on body parts such as the top of the head, a shoulder, or an elbow.

Curriculum Connections: Both body-part identification and balance are *science* concepts.

Ready, Set, Action!

This activity requires a tiny bit of delayed gratification, which contributes to children's self-regulation.

To Have: No materials needed

To Do: Speaking slowly, give the children a short list of movements to do—but ask them to wait until you've stopped speaking before they start doing the actions. Here are a few possible action sequences:

- Jump twice, then shake all over.
- Clap twice, then give yourself a hug.
- Bend and straighten, then reach up high.

More to Do: When the children are ready, present them with some three-part sequences, such as blink your eyes, then clap twice, and then turn around in a circle.

Curriculum Connections: Active listening and word comprehension are both part of *emergent literacy*. Sequencing is an element of *math*.

Imitating Movement

This activity is similar to The Mirror Game, in which the children act as your reflection as you perform a variety of movements one at a time. But, like Ready, Set, Action! this game requires some delayed gratification.

To Have: No materials needed

To Do: Perform a short sequence of movements at a slow to moderate speed, without saying anything. When you've completed the sequence, the children imitate it. Here are some possible sequences:

- Bend your knees, straighten your knees, and then put your hands on your hips.
- Rise up on your tiptoes, lower your heels, and then clap your hands twice.
- Bend forward at the waist, straighten up, and then place your hands on your head.
- Jump twice in place, open and close your mouth, and then shake your arms.

More to Do: When the children are ready for more challenging sequences, simply add to them!

Curriculum Connections: The ability to physically replicate what the eyes see is central to *art* and to *emergent literacy* (writing), while sequencing is a *math* concept.

Freeze Tag

To Have: No materials needed

To Do: Designate one player to be it. This player's assignment is to tag other players. Once a player is tagged, she must remain frozen, feet apart, until another player crawls under her legs! If it can freeze everybody, the last person tagged gets to be it in the next round.

Curriculum Connections: Discuss the concept of freezing with the children to link this game to *science*. You might also want to talk with the children about the muscle tension involved in acting frozen, which is also science.

Shadow Tag

To Have: A sunny day

To Do: Explain to the children that this game is similar to Freeze Tag but involves the child who's it tagging players by stepping on their shadow. When a child is tagged in this way, she's frozen until another player steps on her shadow and frees her.

Curriculum Connections: The concept of shadows falls under the content area of *science*.

Alphabet Tag

To Have: No materials needed

To Do: Designate one player to be it. This player's assignment is to tag other players. When tagged, a player must take on the shape of a letter and remain frozen in that shape until another player approaches and correctly identifies the letter. The formerly frozen player can then rejoin the game.

Curriculum Connections: This is an experience in *emergent literacy*.

Finding a Balance

Balance requires a great deal of self-control, but doing an activity like this makes children realize that self-control can be fun!

To Have: No materials needed

To Do: Challenge the children to balance by holding as still as possible on the following body parts while you count to five:

- hands and knees
- hands and feet
- knees and elbows
- feet and bottom
- hands and bottom

More to Do: When you think the children are ready, ask them to balance on their bottom, knees, or toes only.

Another variation of this activity is to simply ask the children to find a way to balance on a certain number of body parts. Start with a higher number—say, five—before asking them to balance on fewer body parts.

Curriculum Connections: Balance and body-part identification are both *science* concepts. The counting brings in *math*.

Mother, May I?

The traditional version of this game may encourage favoritism, and it involves a great deal of waiting for the children. This alternate version remedies those problems.

To Have: No materials needed

To Do: You take the role of Mother. Stand facing the children, about twenty feet away. Give an instruction for the children to do a certain number of a certain kind of movements. For example, you might say, "Children, take five steps forward on tiptoe." Or, "Children, take three jumps backward." Before doing as directed, the children ask, "Mother, may I?" The game continues until the children reach you. You can then start over with someone else acting as Mother.

Curriculum Connections: Counting is a *math* activity, while active listening falls under *emergent literacy*.

What's the Time, Mr. Dog?

This is a less competitive version of the more traditional, What's the Time, Mr. Wolf?, which involves one of the children being caught.

To Have: No materials needed

To Do: Acting as the dog, stand with your back to the children, about twenty feet away. The children, pretending to be cats, begin sneaking up on you, periodically asking, "What's the time, Mr. Dog?" You then turn around and give a time (any time will do). As soon as you turn around, the children must remain completely still. If you turn around and say, "Dinnertime!" you start chasing the cats, who must run back to the starting line, where they're safe from the dog. You can then start the game all over again, with someone else playing the dog.

Curriculum Connections: The concept of time falls under the heading of *math*, while considering animals constitutes *science*.

Let's Sit

Although sitting is a skill the children have probably long since mastered, it can still be a challenging activity when explored in the following ways. This activity is performed on the floor (no chairs).

To Have: No materials needed

To Do: Present the following challenges to the children:

- Sit from a standing position, using your hands to let you down.

- Do it again, only this time without using your hands.

- Sit down very slowly.

- Sit with a thump.

- Sit with your weight on just one thigh (hip).

- From a kneeling position, sit down gently.

- From a kneeling position, sit down with a thump.

- Sit up from a lying position.

- Show me how slowly you can sit up from a lying position.

Curriculum Connections: This activity moves the children through different vertical levels in space, which can be linked to both *art* and *math*.

Shrinking Room

This activity helps children understand that they take their personal space with them when they move around—and that they should respect others' personal space.

To Have: One plastic hoop per child (optional)

To Do: Ask each child to step inside a plastic hoop, pick it up, and put it around her waist. (If you don't have enough hoops for everyone, ask the children to stand with their arms out to their sides.) Then challenge the children to imagine they're each either inside a giant bubble or that they're driving cars on the highway (which- ever image you think will work best with your group). Invite the children to move around the room without touching anyone else's bubble or car (hoop or hands).

Stand with your arms out to your sides, acting as a "wall" beyond which the children can't pass. Gradually begin reducing the size of the area in which the children have to move, reminding them if necessary that they still mustn't touch one another. Be sure to stop "shrinking the room" while the children are still able to move around without touching another person's hoop or hands!

Curriculum Connections: If you're using cars for imagery, you're bringing in trans- portation and therefore *social studies*. If you use the idea of bubbles, you're address- ing *science*.

Roll Around

This is both a cooperative activity and a self-regulation activity. It takes a *lot* of self- control and concentration, but the children will exhibit both because they enjoy meeting this particular challenge.

To Have: A parachute or large sheet and a small ball

To Do: Have the children stand around the parachute and hold it with both hands. Place the ball on the parachute. Ask the children to show you they can work together to get the ball to roll around the outer edge—first in one direction and then in the other direction.

Curriculum Connections: A sense of direction is essential to reading and writing (*emergent literacy*), while the momentum explored here is a *science* concept. *Math* is also involved as the children experience moving the ball around the circumfer- ence of the circle or the perimeter of the sheet.

Moving Backward

Once the children have acquired a respect for personal space, they should be ready for this activity, which requires a great deal of self-control.

To Have: No materials needed

To Do: Invite the children to move backward in the following ways (reminding them to look over their shoulders):

- walking
- jumping
- walking with little steps
- walking with big steps
- tiptoeing

Curriculum Connections: Big and little are quantitative concepts, which fall under the content area of *math*; they're also adjectives, making them part of *emergent literacy*. Direction is a component of *art* and *math* but is also essential to reading and writing (*emergent literacy*).

Balance and Recover

To Have: No materials needed

To Do: Challenge the children to achieve balance using the bases of support listed below. In each of these balances, they are to see how far they can lean *before* falling over. They then return to their original positions. Encourage them to lean forward, backward, and to each side.

Here are some possible bases of support:

- both feet (flat)
- both feet on tiptoe
- one foot (flat)
- on tiptoe with knees bent
- on tiptoe with eyes closed
- both knees
- one knee
- their bottoms

Curriculum Connections: Balance is a *science* concept.

Brain Breaks

There are numerous reasons, including preventing restlessness and off-task behavior, for getting the children up and moving after they've been sitting for a while. Both children and adults learn better and more quickly when their efforts are distributed (breaks are included) than when their efforts are concentrated (work is conducted in longer periods). Because young children don't process information as effectively as older children and adults do, due to the immaturity of young children's nervous systems and their lack of experience, they gain the most benefit from taking breaks.

In 2016 psychologist Karrie E. Godwin and her colleagues studied how attentive elementary school students were while in class. These researchers discovered that the children spent more than a quarter of their time distracted and unable to focus on either the teacher or the task at hand. However, when children received their lessons in ten-minute periods, as opposed to thirty-minute periods, attention improved (Godwin et al. 2016).

Finland has taken the research on this subject to heart. Schools in Finland offer their students a fifteen-minute recess, during which the children usually go outdoors to play and socialize, *after every forty-five minutes of instruction.* What is more: Finnish schools have a shorter school day than US schools do. This approach seems to be working, as Finland's successes in literacy and numeracy have teachers visiting from all over the world to learn that country's secrets.

American teacher Timothy Walker has had firsthand experience with this facet of Finnish education. When he moved to Finland and began teaching there, at first he felt the Finnish way was "soft" and was "convinced that kids learned better with longer stretches of instructional time." Walker decided to skip the fifteen-minute breaks, opting instead to teach two forty-five-minute lessons back-to-back, followed by a double break of thirty minutes. On his third day of teaching, one of his young students rebelled, claiming that he was about to "explode" (Walker 2017, 9–10).

Walker wisely took some time to reflect. He realized that his American approach hadn't actually worked very well in the United States either. His students had typically experienced a slump in energy after forty-five minutes in class. So he began offering his Finnish students the short breaks with which they were familiar, and his students remained fresh throughout the day. He writes, "I remembered that Finns have known this for years—they've been providing breaks to their students since the 1960s" (Walker 2017, 10).

In the United States, on the other hand, the research is being ignored. According to the American Association for the Child's Right to Play (www.ipausa.org), approximately 40 percent of elementary schools have jettisoned recess—the ultimate brain break. The rationale is typically so that children can receive more instructional time (IPA/USA, accessed 2019). But instructional time without breaks is counterproductive.

Researcers Olga S. Jarrett and Darlene M. Maxwell determined that recess increases focus, among other things. They approached an urban school district that had a no-recess policy and received permission for two fourth-grade classes to have recess once a week so they could observe the children's behavior on recess and non-recess days. Their results showed that the forty-three children became more on-task and less fidgety on days when they had recess (Jarrett and Maxwell 2000).

Additionally, studies show that human brains aren't inactive while people are taking a break from learning. Rather, brains are actually processing information and making sense of what they've experienced. Neuroscientist Mary Helen Immordino-Yang writes (2016, 60), "Rest is indeed not idleness, nor is it a wasted opportunity for productivity."

While you may not be able to follow the example Finland has set, you can be sure that regular brain breaks are an important part of the children's experience in your setting. Noted educator Eric Jensen has said that the learning brain can absorb information for only a handful of minutes at a time. He explains that a physical activity break provides the brain with a boost of norepinephrine, an "upper" for the brain, and dopamine, which helps support working memory. And, of course, he's also written that sitting for more than ten minutes at a time increases fatigue and reduces concentration, both of which increase discipline problems (Jensen 2000, 30).

Brain breaks not only wake up the brain and prevent excessive fidgeting and fatigue, they also promote a sense of fun and make your setting somewhere that the children want to be! Author and physical educator Cathie Summerford tells us they aren't "throwaway activities" to be "randomly inserted" into the schedule. Rather, she writes, "They are purposeful interludes that you use strategically." She feels kids are likely to be "de-energized . . . when a long lesson begins to drag" (Summerford 2009, 21).

Jensen and Summerford refer to these brief exercises as energizers. Some have taken to calling them brain boosters. But the most popular term is *brain breaks*, so that's the term I'm using here. The activities that follow, in addition to stimulating mind and body, provide opportunities for the children to solve problems, use their imagination, develop body and spatial awareness, and experience word comprehension (emergent literacy), mathematics, and science concepts in a brain-friendly way. The activities also provide practice with certain locomotor and nonlocomotor skills—practice that is necessary for children to gain competence and confidence in their physical abilities, which are important if children are to achieve lifelong health.

These activities require little to no equipment. Many can be performed in one spot. And don't forget: you'll find more options for brain breaks under other categories in this book!

Walkabout

To Have: No materials needed

To Do: Invite the children to walk in the following ways:

- in place while standing straight and tall
- with knees lifted high
- with tiny steps
- with giant steps
- step-step-stop (repeat)
- forward on the heels
- backward on tiptoe
- sideways while making their bodies very small
- quickly and zigzagging
- as quickly and lightly as possible
- in slow motion back to their seats

Curriculum Connections: Directionality and spatial awareness are very much a part of reading and writing (*emergent literacy*), as are adjectives such as *quickly* and *lightly*.

Up and Down We Go

To Have: No materials needed

To Do: Present the children with the following challenges:

- Show me with your body what *up* and *down* mean.

- Show me you can make your body go all the way down.

- Show me you can make your body go all the way up.

- How high up can you get?

- Show me you can go down halfway.

- How low can you go?

- Pretend your feet are glued to the floor and show me you can move your body up and down without moving your feet.

- Pretend you're toast coming out of the toaster.

- Show me you can look like popcorn popping.

- Show me you can look like a bouncing ball.

- Pretend you are a balloon inflating and deflating.

Curriculum Connections: Up, down, and halfway are *math* concepts, as are the quantitative concepts of high and low.

Head, Shoulders, Knees, and Toes

To Have: No materials needed

To Do: Ask the children to touch their heads, shoulders, knees, and toes as you call out the name of these body parts. Once the children are experiencing success with this, reverse—and mix up—the order of the body parts you call out. You can also vary the tempo at which you call out body parts or start out slowly and gradually accelerate.

Curriculum Connections: Body-part identification is an introductory *science* concept. Listening skills are part of *emergent literacy*.

Body-Part Break

To Have: No materials needed

To Do: Call out the name of various body parts, asking the children to show the designated body parts to you. Start with those most familiar to the children.

Once you've addressed familiar body parts, move on to more challenging ones, like ankles, wrists, thighs, and shins.

Eventually begin increasing the tempo at which you call out the body parts. The children love this!

Curriculum Connections: Body-part identification falls under the content area of *science* for young children. If you vary the tempo at which you call out body parts, you'll be introducing the children to an element of *music*.

Bend and Stretch

To Have: No materials needed

To Do: Invite the children to do the following actions, which contribute to the fitness factor of flexibility:

- Stretch as though picking fruit from a tall tree.

- Flop like you're a rag doll.

- Stretch as though you're waking up and yawning first thing in the morning.

- Bend as though to tie your shoes.

- Stretch as if to put something on a high shelf.

- Bend as if to pat a dog, an even smaller dog, then a cat.

- Stretch as if to shoot a basketball through a hoop.

- Bend as if you're picking up a coin from the floor.

- Stretch as though reaching for a star.

Curriculum Connections: If you discuss up, down, high, and low, you link this activity to *math*. If you talk about lengthening the muscles during stretching and the action of the joints involved in bending, you bring in *science*.

Running in Place

To Have: No materials needed

To Do: Invite the children to do the following activities. These activities contribute to the fitness factor of cardiovascular endurance:

- Jog in your own little space.
- Show me you can do it with your knees going higher.
- Show me you can jog faster.
- Show me you can jog slower.
- Jog in a little circle.
- Run in place, making a lot of noise with your feet.
- Jog and stop on my signal.
- Jog very lightly in place, with tiny steps.

Curriculum Connections: Children who have no sense of personal space tend to write with their letters crowded together, so experiences with personal space contribute to *emergent literacy*, as do the adjectives and adverbs involved. There are also *math* concepts, such as a higher position and the shape of a circle, included in this activity.

Giants and Elves

To Have: No materials needed

To Do: Read the following poem in its entirety, explaining anything you feel needs clarification. Then divide the children into "giants" and "elves" and read the poem line by line, having the children act out their roles accordingly. If time permits, repeat the activity with the children reversing roles.

See the giants, great and tall,
Hear them bellow, hear them call.
Life looks different from up so high,
With head and shoulders clear to the sky.
And at their feet they can barely see
The little people so very tiny,
Who scurry about with hardly a care
Avoiding enormous feet placed here and there.
But together they dwell, the giants and elves,
In peace and harmony among themselves.

Curriculum Connections: The poem incorporates several quantitative concepts, such as high, big, little, and together, making it a *math* experience. A poem is also an experience in *emergent literacy*, as is the exploration of opposites such as tiny and enormous.

Shake It

To Have: No materials needed

To Do: Challenge the children to do the following:

- Shake your whole body all over.

- Shake just one hand, then the other hand, then both together.

- Shake your hands in front of you, to either side, up high, and down low.

- Find another part of your body to shake, then another.

- When kneeling, how many parts of your body can you shake?

Curriculum Connections: Body-part identification is part of *science*, while the positional concepts involved bring in *math*.

Shake It Again

To Have: No materials needed

To Do: Discuss the meanings of the words *shaking*, *wiggling*, and *vibrating* with the children. Then invite them to do the following:

- Move like soup when the bowl is shaken.

- Wiggle like a snake.

- Shake and vibrate like a baby's rattle.

- Shake like a leaf on a tree blowing in the wind.

- Shiver as though you are very, very cold.

- Vibrate like a battery-powered toothbrush.

Curriculum Connections: The word comprehension involved in this activity falls into the category of *emergent literacy*. The self-expression involved ties the activity to *social studies*.

Light and Heavy

To Have: No materials needed

To Do: Invite the children to sit on the floor and tap their fingers lightly on the floor in front of them. Next, ask them to pound their fists on the floor.

Continue alternating between the two, varying the amount of time the children get to do each. Point out the contrast between the light and heavy movements of the children's hands.

More to Do: Later you can ask the children to move as lightly as possible around the room, imagining they're walking on eggs and trying not to break them. Then invite the children to move heavily, making as much noise with their feet as they can. Continue to alternate between the two.

Curriculum Connections: Light and heavy are quantitative concepts, which makes them part of *math*.

Rabbits and 'Roos

To Have: No materials needed

To Do: Talk to the children about rabbits and kangaroos, asking them to tell you about some of the differences between these animals. Which is bigger? Which is smaller? Which would jump more heavily? Which would jump more lightly?

Invite the children to move first like one animal and then like the other. Alternate between the two, using the words *small*, *big*, *light*, and *heavy* to describe what the children are doing. You can also point out how low or high their jumps are.

Curriculum Connections: Big, small, light, heavy, low, and high are all quantitative concepts, placing this activity in the content area of *math*.

Making Shapes

To Have: No materials needed

To Do: Present the following challenges to the children:

- Show me how round you can be.

- Show me how flat (wide, narrow, long, short, crooked, or straight) you can be.

- Show me you can make your body look like a table, then a chair.

- Show me you can look like a ball (a pencil with a point at the end, a flower, or a teapot).

Curriculum Connections: Shape is an element of both *art* and *math*, which is further explored with the quantitative concepts of wide, narrow, long, and short.

Touch It

To Have: No materials needed

To Do: Call out a shape or a color. The children locate a possibility in the room, move to it, touch it, and then return to stand by their desk or original spot. Repeat with more shapes or colors.

Curriculum Connections: Shape and color are components of *art*. Shape is also part of geometry (*math*).

Skywriting

To Have: Letters posted where the children can see them

To Do: Ask the children to choose a letter they would like to write (or assign one). Then have the children "write" their letters in the air in front of them, making the letters as large as possible. Repeat this several times, asking the children to keep making their letters a bit smaller each time. Continue in this manner with a variety of letters.

More to Do: You can later ask the children to write letters with the following body parts:

- an elbow

- a knee

- the top of the head

- the nose

- a big toe (on the floor)

Curriculum Connections: A focus on the straight and curving lines that make up letters constitutes *emergent literacy*, while body-part awareness falls under the heading of *science*.

It's Geometric

To Have: Construction paper cutouts or pictures of different shapes, such as squares, triangles, circles, and rectangles (optional)

To Do: Show the children the cutouts or point out these shapes in the room. Then invite the children to replicate the shapes one at a time with their bodies.

Curriculum Connections: This is all about *math.*

Stand Up, Sit Down

To Have: No materials needed

To Do: Present the following challenges. Feel free to add to these:

- Stand up if you're wearing blue.
- Sit down if you're a boy.
- Stand up if you have a dog at home.
- Sit down if you have a cat at home.
- Stand up if you have a bird at home.
- Sit down if you have blond hair.
- Stand up if you have brown eyes.
- Sit down if you're a girl.
- Stand up if you're wearing green.
- Sit down if you can hear me.

Curriculum Connections: Because this activity involves active listening, it falls under the content area of *emergent literacy.*

A Pair of . . .

To Have: No materials needed

To Do: Explain that a pair means a set of two objects that belong together, such as a pair of shoes. Ask the children to point to the various pairs of body parts they have. Here are some possibilities:

eyes	hands	elbows
ears	feet	knees

legs	pointer fingers	nostrils
shoulders	thumbs	wrists
arms	pinky fingers	

More to Do: Following this, you might ask the children to move around the room looking for pairs. Possibilities include a pair of shoes or mittens, a pair of markers at the whiteboard, a pair of plants on a windowsill, or a pair of windows.

Curriculum Connections: The concept of a pair falls under the content area of *math*, while the body-part identification belongs under *science*.

Exploring Opposites

To Have: No materials needed

To Do: Talk to the children about the meaning of the word *opposites*. Then explain that you're going to give them an instruction to do something. They will respond by doing what you asked. You will then instruct them to do the opposite.

Here are some possible challenges:

- Make yourself very tall (short).
- Show me how high (low) you can go.
- Show me tiny (giant) steps.
- Move as though you're very sad (happy).
- Move lightly (heavily).
- Show me how quickly (slowly) you can move.

Curriculum Connections: The concept of opposites is part of *emergent literacy*, as are the adjectives and adverbs involved here.

Same Length

To Have: No materials needed

To Do: Invite the children to move around the room searching for objects that are the same length (just as long) as their hands. How many such objects can they find?

More to Do: An alternative is to ask the children to search for objects that are the same length as their arms or the same length as the distance from their elbows to their wrists.

Curriculum Connections: Length and the concept of how many fall under the content area of *math*.

Let's Sway

To Have: No materials needed

To Do: If necessary, demonstrate swaying to the children, explaining that a sway transfers weight from one part of the body to another in an easy, relaxed motion. Invite the children to try swaying from side to side and then back and forth.

Now add some imagery to the activity, asking the children to sway like the following objects:

- flowers in the breeze
- bells ringing
- rocking horses (or rocking chairs)
- windshield wipers

Curriculum Connections: The self-expression involved contributes to *social studies*. To bring in *science*, discuss the fact that swaying requires muscles to be relaxed.

Let's Jump

To Have: No materials needed

To Do: Remind the children that a jump starts with two feet on the ground propelling the body upward. Invite the children to jump in place in the following ways:

- with their feet barely coming off the floor
- with their feet coming way off the floor
- with their knees going as high as possible
- while being as tall as they can
- making a lot of noise with their feet
- as lightly as possible

Curriculum Connections: Positional concepts are part of *math*.

Jumping for Joy

To Have: No materials needed

To Do: Invite the children to do the following:

- Jump as though you're a bouncing ball (sometimes high, sometimes low).

- Jump as if you are reaching for something high above you.

- Jump as though you're startled by a loud noise.

- Jump as if you're angry.

- Jump for joy!

Curriculum Connections: High and low are positional concepts that fall under the heading of *math*. The self-expression and exploration of emotions involved in this activity fall under the content area of *social studies*.

"Pop Goes the Weasel"

To Have: No materials needed

To Do: Invite the children to walk around the room or outdoor area while you hum or sing "Pop Goes the Weasel." Every time the students hear the "pop," they jump lightly into the air.

More to Do: To make this activity more challenging, invite the children to do the following:

- Change direction with each pop.

- Clap and jump with each pop.

- Do both of the above at the same time.

Curriculum Connections: The song brings in *music*, while the active listening is part of *emergent literacy*.

Above, Below, and On

To Have: One jump rope per child (or lines on the floor)

To Do: Each child places the rope flat on the floor in a horizontal line (or stands behind a line on the floor). You then call out the words *above, below,* or *on,* indicating where the children should stand in relation to the rope or line. Call out the words in various orders and at various speeds.

Curriculum Connections: These positional concepts are part of early geometry, which places them under the content area of *math*. Because children must learn to write their letters above, below, and on lines on paper, this also qualifies as an experience in *emergent literacy*.

Do a Little Dance

To Have: A piece of lively recorded music

To Do: Start the music and invite the children to get up from their seats and move in whatever way they want—in one spot. If you have some children who feel self-conscious about improvising in this way, you can suggest that they do the silliest dance they can. Another possibility is to invite them to "dance" individual body parts, such as fingers, elbows, or knees.

Curriculum Connections: This activity involves both *music* and *science* (body-part identification).

Advanced Jumping

To Have: No materials needed

To Do: Challenge the children to try the following:

- Jump with your feet together.
- Jump with your feet apart.
- Jump with your feet alternately apart and together.
- Land with one foot forward and the other behind.
- Jump with your arms folded across your chest.

- Jump with your hands on your hips.

- Jump and clap at the same time.

- Make a funny shape with your body while you're in the air.

Curriculum Connections: Together, forward, and behind are *math* concepts.

More Bending and Stretching

To Have: No materials needed

To Do: Invite the children to perform the following:

- Show me you can stretch one arm high and the other low (one toward the ceiling and the other toward the floor).

- Bend one arm while stretching the other arm high, low, or out to the side.

- Reach both arms to the right (or to one side), then to the left (to the other side).

- Reach one arm to the side and the other toward the ceiling.

- Find out how many other body parts can be bent or stretched!

Curriculum Connections: The positional concepts involved are part of the content area of *math*, as is the quantitative concept of how many. Exploring the capabilities and limitations of body parts constitutes *science*.

Let's Turn

To Have: No materials needed

To Do: Present the following challenges:

- Turn yourself around to the right. Now turn to the left.

- Turn yourself around very, very slowly.

- Turn while making yourself as tall as you can, then while making yourself as small as you can.

- Jump and turn at the same time.

- Jump and turn in the other direction.

Curriculum Connections: Directionality is critical to reading and writing, meaning this activity links to *emergent literacy*.

Let's Turn Again

To Have: No materials needed

To Do: Invite the children to try these more difficult turning challenges:

- Hop and turn at the same time.
- Turn while making yourself as round as you can be.
- Turn while making yourself as crooked as you can be.
- Turn on only one foot.
- Turn on the other foot.

Curriculum Connections: The concepts of roundness and crookedness are *math* concepts. So is the quantity of one.

Let's March

To Have: Recorded marching music (optional)

To Do: Invite the children to march in the following ways:

- in place, raising knees high
- in place, turning in one direction, then in place, turning in the other direction
- as though playing an instrument you might see in a marching band
- as if carrying a flag in a parade
- with knees high and arms swinging
- around the room or playground

Curriculum Connections: If you use a recorded march, you'll bring *music* into the mix. To bring in *social studies*, talk about the occasions on which there might be parades.

Walk on the Wild Side

To Have: No materials needed

To Do: Invite the children to walk either in place or around the indoor or outdoor area as though they're in the following situations:

- on slippery ice
- on hot sand that's burning their feet
- in deep snow

- in sticky mud
- weightless in outer space
- in a jungle with thick growth
- on a busy, crowded sidewalk

Curriculum Connections: The self-expression involved in this activity brings in *social studies*. If you discuss any of the aspects of the environments mentioned, you'll address *science* concepts.

Walk with Feeling

To Have: No materials needed

To Do: Invite the children to walk either in place or around the indoor or outdoor area, demonstrating the following emotions:

- tired
- angry

- sad
- proud

- scared
- happy

Curriculum Connections: Identifying and expressing emotions falls under the content area of early childhood *social studies*.

Let's Push and Pull

To Have: No materials needed

To Do: Talk to the children about the difference between pushing and pulling, then issue the following challenges:

- Show me how you would push a swing.
- Show me how you would pull a rope.
- Show me how you would push heavy furniture.

- Pretend to pull a kite.
- Pretend to push a balloon into the air.
- Pretend to pull an anchor out of the water.

- Pretend to push a car stuck in mud or snow.

- Pretend to pull in a game of tug-of-war.

- Pretend to push a shovel.

- Pretend to pull a balloon down from the sky.

Curriculum Connections: There are varying levels of muscle tension required for these tasks. If you talk to the children about this, you'll be bringing in *science*. The self-expression required involves *social studies*.

How Many Steps?

To Have: No materials needed

To Do: The children line up side by side on one end of the room. Invite them to count how many steps it takes to get to the other side. (Remind the children that because they may take steps of varying sizes, there is no one right answer.)

Curriculum Connections: Counting and the concept of how many are a part of *math*.

Let's Strike

To Have: No materials needed

To Do: Ask the children to pretend to be doing the following:

- playing a big bass drum in a marching band

- hammering a nail

- chopping wood

- swatting at a mosquito

- hitting a ball with a bat

Curriculum Connections: Talk to the children about some of the professions involved in these tasks to bring in *social studies*. If you discuss the muscle tension involved in these striking activities, you'll be addressing *science*.

The Mirror Game

To Have: No materials needed

To Do: Standing where all the children can see you easily, explain that they should pretend to be your reflection in a mirror, imitating your every move. Then move parts of your body in various ways, such as the following:

- raising and lowering an arm
- tilting your head
- lifting and lowering a knee
- placing your hands on your hips

- raising your arms overhead
- shaking all over
- nodding your head
- bending and straightening at the waist

Curriculum Connections: This activity involves creating various shapes with the body, and the concept of shape is part of both *art* and *math*.

Going on a Treasure Hunt

To Have: Several items linked by a unifying theme (for example, stuffed animals, plastic eggs, or plastic farm animals) and a basket or bag for each child

To Do: Before you do this activity, you will need to hide the items you've chosen throughout the room. You then tell the children what you've hidden and invite them to go in search of the items, collecting them as they go. When a predetermined amount of time has passed (perhaps five minutes), bring the children back to the center of the room, where they empty the contents of their bags and count their own items.

Curriculum Connections: Counting makes this a *math* experience.

I Spy

To Have: No materials needed

To Do: Chant "I spy with my little eye . . . ," concluding your sentence with a color, a type of line (diagonal, vertical, horizontal, and so on), or perhaps a shape (round, crooked, square, and so on). The children then look around the room, moving to whatever they believe it might be (it's always best if there's more than one possibility). Repeat several times.

Curriculum Connections: If you're spying a type of line, you'll be making this a *math* experience. If you choose a color, it will be an *art* experience. And if you choose shapes, the activity will fall under both math and art.

High and Low

To Have: A kazoo (optional)

To Do: Using your humming voice or a kazoo, start with a low note and gradually get higher and higher, inviting the children to accompany the pitch with arm movements, starting with their arms down low and raising them as the notes ascend.

Once you've gone as high in pitch as you can, reverse the process. Have the children lower their arms with the descending notes.

More to Do: When the children are familiar with this process, ask them to crouch low to the floor or ground and do this with their whole bodies.

Curriculum Connections: This brain break is a great active listening activity, making it part of *emergent literacy*. High and low are quantitative concepts falling under the content area of *math*.

What Goes Up Must Come Down

To Have: No materials needed

To Do: Invite the children to do the following movements:

- Crouch near the floor and then rise up, with your head leading the way.

- Go back down with your elbow leading the way.

- Come up from the floor with your elbow leading.

- Go back down with your nose leading the way.

- Rise back up with your nose leading.

- Go back down with your chest leading.

- Come back up with your chin leading.

- Go back down to your seat with your bottom leading the way.

Curriculum Connections: This activity reinforces the concepts of up and down (*math*), while also offering practice with body-part identification, a *science* concept.

Let's Lift

To Have: No materials needed

To Do: Ask the children to show you what it would look like to lift the following things:

- a big heavy rock
- a big beach ball
- a chair
- a log

- a basket
- a balloon
- the handles of a wheelbarrow
- a container filled to the brim with liquid

Curriculum Connections: If you talk about the difference in muscle tension or force required to lift these various items, you bring *science* into the mix. If you relate it to differences in size and weight, *math* is involved.

Cross-Crawl

To Have: No materials needed

To Do: You can stand facing the children or with your back to them. In either case, ask the children to mirror what you're doing: alternating right elbow to left knee and left elbow to right knee. Touching the knee with the opposite hand also does the trick!

Curriculum Connections: This Brain Gym activity involves cross-lateral movement and crossing the vertical midline of the body. Both of these types of movements encourage the two hemispheres of the brain to communicate across the corpus callosum, which contributes to ease of reading and writing (*emergent literacy*).

Come to Me

To Have: One carpet square, hoop, poly spot, or other type of personal space marker per child (optional)

To Do: The children stand next to their desks or on or in their personal space markers while you stand in the center of the room where every child can see you. Invite the children to come to you in a variety of ways. For instance, you might say, "Come to me by traveling in a straight line" (on tiptoe, in a crooked shape, stomping your feet, or sideways).

Once the children reach you, give them directions for returning to their desk or personal space, such as, "Return to your personal space in a curving line."

Curriculum Connections: This activity reinforces spatial relationships, making it part of both *math* and *emergent literacy*.

Traveling Body Parts

To Have: No materials needed

To Do: Invite the children to do the following:

- Make one hand travel far away from the other one.

- Leaving the first hand (the one that traveled) where it is, bring the other hand to meet it.

- Make the first hand travel far away from the other one but in a different direction.

- Make one elbow travel far away from the other one.

- Leaving the first elbow where it is, bring the other elbow to meet it.

- Make the first elbow travel far away again, but in a different direction.

Curriculum Connections: This activity is excellent for helping children understand the realm of their personal space. Children who have little or no sense of their own personal space often write their letters in a crowded, jumbled manner. This activity, therefore, can contribute to *emergent literacy*. Because it also requires identifying body parts and their capabilities and limitations, *science* is involved too.

Let's Swing

To Have: No materials needed

To Do: Invite the children to try the following actions:

- Swing your arms back and forth.

- Show me you can swing your arms slower, then quicker.

- Swing your arms from side to side.

- Swing your head from side to side, as though it were a windshield wiper.

- Swing your body as if you were on a flying trapeze.

- Swing your arms like an elephant's trunk.

Curriculum Connections: Identifying body parts and their capabilities and limitations constitutes a *science* experience. Swinging also involves momentum, another science concept.

Let's Swing Some More

To Have: No materials needed

To Do: Present the following challenges to the children:

- With your arms hanging loosely and heavily from your shoulders, swing them back and forth in a small arc.

- Show me you can swing your arms a little more.

- Swing your arms from side to side.

- Bend forward a little, letting your arms hang down. Show me you can swing them forward and backward.

- Swing them from side to side, starting with a small arc and gradually increasing in size.

Curriculum Connections: As above, *science* is involved in two ways: identifying body parts and their capabilities and limitations and exploring the concept of momentum.

Exploring Right and Left

To Have: No materials needed

To Do: Stand facing the children, pointing out to them when they're working with their right and left sides, using your opposite side to act as a mirror reflection. Then perform the following movements, one side at a time:

- Raise and lower an arm.
- Move an arm in a smooth, wavy way.
- Lift a leg forward, then put it back on the floor.
- Lift a leg to the side and put it back.
- Wiggle the fingers on one hand.
- Bend a knee.
- Put a hand on a hip.

Curriculum Connections: Reading and writing involve moving the eyes and hand, respectively, from left to right, so an understanding of laterality contributes to *emergent literacy*. This is also a body-part-identification activity, so *science* is involved as well.

Doing the Twist

To Have: No materials needed

To Do: Invite the students to twist in the following ways:

- like the inside of a washing machine
- like a screwdriver when someone is using it
- like a wet dishrag being wrung
- as though wiping their bottom with a towel
- as though digging a little hole in the sand with a foot
- as though wiping with a towel and digging a hole in the sand with a foot at the same time

Curriculum Connections: The self-expression involved here means this is a *social studies* experience.

Changing It Up

This activity involves three different locomotor skills (all performed in place) and the movement elements of space, shape, force, flow, and time.

To Have: No materials needed

To Do: Challenge the children to perform the following actions:

- Walk in place.
- Jump in a little circle.
- Run in place with knees high and arms low.
- Jump as hard as you can.
- Walk in place as lightly as you can.
- Jump-jump-stop, then repeat.
- Walk in place as quickly as you can.
- Run in place, making yourself as tall as you can.
- Walk in place as slowly as you can.

Curriculum Connections: Experience with the adjectives and adverbs involved here contributes to *emergent literacy*. The concepts of high, low, and lightly fall under the content area of *math*.

Body-Part Balance

To Have: No materials needed

To Do: Ask the children to place the following body parts—and only those body parts—on the floor:

- hands and knees
- knees alone
- hands and feet
- knees and elbows
- just their bottom
- just their feet

Curriculum Connections: Both body-part identification and balance come under the content area of *science*.

Body-Part Balance II

To Have: No materials needed

To Do: Ask the children to balance on five, four, three, two, and one body part(s), respectively, challenging them to find at least two solutions to each combination. For example, a challenge to place weight on one body part could result in standing on the right or left foot, sitting on their bottoms, or balancing on one or the other knee.

Curriculum Connections: Both body-part identification and balance come under the content area of *science*. The counting of body parts brings in *math*.

In My Own Space

To Have: No materials needed

To Do: Challenge the children to first perform the following nonlocomotor skills with the whole body and then to find different body parts also capable of performing these skills:

- bend
- swing
- bounce
- stretch
- shake
- twist

Curriculum Connections: Exploring the capabilities and limitations of body parts falls under the heading of *science*.

Hopping in Place

To Have: No materials needed

To Do: Explain that a hop takes off from and lands on just one foot. Then invite the children to hop in place on the preferred foot (it's okay to hold on to a chair or table if they want to). They should then try hopping on the nonpreferred foot.

More to Do: When the children are comfortable with hopping, ask them to hop both lightly and heavily, then both quickly and slowly.

Curriculum Connections: Lightly, heavily, quickly, and slowly are *math* concepts. These words are also adverbs, which means they fall under the heading of *emergent literacy*.

Opposing Body Halves

To Have: No materials needed

To Do: Explain that the right side of the body can do a task separate from the left side. So can the top of the body and the bottom. Then pose the following challenges:

- Make a slow movement with one arm and then a fast movement with the other. Switch sides.

- Make a gentle, light movement with one arm and then a strong, hard movement with the other. Switch.

- Make a slow, light movement with your arms and hands, followed by a fast, hard movement with your legs and feet. Switch.

Curriculum Connections: Several adjectives are involved in this activity, making it an experience in *emergent literacy*. Because the children will also be identifying and experimenting with body parts, *science* is also addressed.

Relaxation Exercises

Stress is a normal part of life, but in our current society we are seeing increasing levels of stress and anxiety among children (Bitsko et al. 2018). It's critical that children be able to calm themselves, but adults may not realize that relaxation is a learned skill. As with any significant life skill, early childhood is the time to begin learning it.

Relaxation is important for children for numerous reasons. Among them is the research showing that stress is detrimental to learning, so relaxation techniques can help improve a child's early education experiences (Vogel and Schwabe 2016). Moreover, by calming the nervous system and loosening muscles, relaxation exercises promote better sleep and boost the immune system (Breus 2017).

The late Clare Cherry (1981, viii), in her book *Think of Something Quiet*, wrote that being able to relax can make serenity a part of children's lives, helping them learn "they can be in control of their own bodies and feelings rather than having to let their bodies and feelings control them." This, of course, is a big part of self-regulation.

Children have the opportunity to experience motionlessness—something for which they get too little practice in their everyday lives—and to understand its contrast to movement when they use relaxation techniques. This awareness helps prepare children for slow and sustained movement, which requires greater control than does fast movement. This too is part of self-regulation. All these benefits of relaxation help ensure fewer behavioral issues.

In addition to the relaxation exercises offered here, there are other simple activities that typically calm children. Coloring is one of them, as long as there's no pressure whatsoever to color in a certain way. Coloring and drawing with no expectations can focus children's attention and can be very soothing, particularly if you dim the lights a bit and perhaps play some peaceful music. Similarly, kneading playdough or putty can help children de-stress.

You can use relaxation techniques alternately with more vigorous activities to help establish a calm, reliable pace in your setting—or use them anytime the children seem overcharged, to prevent them from bouncing off the walls. And it couldn't hurt to help children wind down a bit before you send them on their way at the end of the day. Families will be grateful, and the children will leave your setting with positive feelings and a desire to return!

Being Balloons

This activity promotes deep breathing through the use of imagery young children can relate to and find fun.

To Have: A balloon (optional)

To Do: Talk to the children about balloons slowly inflating and deflating. Better yet, if you have a balloon available, show them. Also demonstrate inhaling through the nose and exhaling through the mouth.

Invite the children to pretend they are balloons (any color balloon they want to be), slowly inflating by breathing in through their noses. Once fully inflated, they begin to slowly deflate by letting air out through their mouths.

More to Do: An alternative is to perform this activity with the children lying on their backs. They should place their hands on their bellies, which they are imagining as balloons, feeling the balloons fill as they inflate (breathe in) and empty as they deflate (breathe out).

Curriculum Connections: Inflation and deflation are *science* concepts. You can also include a discussion about the lungs as part of the activity to further connect it to science.

Statues and Rag Dolls

Although contracting and releasing the muscles is an age-old relaxation technique, the words *contract* and *release* mean nothing to young children. But you can use imagery that's meaningful to young children to help them develop the ability to contract and release their muscles.

To Have: Pictures of a statue and a rag doll (optional)

To Do: Talk to the children about statues and rag dolls. Ask them what they think of when they imagine statues and rag dolls. What would it feel like to be a statue? A rag doll?

With the children either lying or standing, ask them to demonstrate, alternately, being a statue and a rag doll. Continue the pattern for a while, always ending with the rag doll.

Curriculum Connections: The contraction and release of muscles makes this a *science* experience.

Contract and Release

We may not be able to instruct children to contract and release muscles, but we can *inspire* them to contract and release muscles by giving them specific assignments. This activity has been adapted from Clare Cherry's book *Think of Something Quiet*.

To Have: No materials needed

To Do: As the children are lying or sitting, invite them to perform the following actions, repeating each two or three times:

- Bring your shoulders as close to your ears as you can. Hold while I count to three, and then let them go.

- Open your mouth as wide as it will go. After I count to three, press your lips together really tightly. After I count to three again, smile.

- Close your eyes and squeeze them really tightly. After I count to three, open them wide.

- Clasp your hands and squeeze your fingers together really tightly. After I count to three, let them go.

- Press the palms of your hands against each other really hard. After I count to three, shake out your hands.

Curriculum Connections: The contraction and release of muscles makes this a *science* experience. The body-part identification further involves science. Counting is an element of *math*.

Push!

To Have: Wall space indoors or outdoors

To Do: Invite the children to find a space at the wall and face the wall. Then ask them to use their whole body—arms, legs, and back muscles—to push against the wall as if trying to move it, while you count to ten. You then count to ten again, during which time the children stop pushing and breathe deeply. Repeat a couple of times, always ending with the breathing.

Curriculum Connections: Resistance and the function of the muscles are *science* concepts, while *math* is addressed with the counting.

Birthday Candles

To Have: No materials needed

To Do: Invite the children to hold up the fingers of one hand. Ask them to imagine that each finger is a candle on a birthday cake. Then, one at a time, they blow out each candle, using a long breath (as opposed to a quick puff). As each candle is extinguished, that finger curls back down toward the palm.

Curriculum Connections: You can add *math* to this activity by counting the five candles, both when they first appear and then one at a time as they disappear. This is also a fine-motor exercise, which will eventually contribute to writing (*emergent literacy*).

Robots and Astronauts

Children love pretending to be robots and astronauts. This activity uses such pretending to promote the contraction and release of muscles.

To Have: No materials needed

To Do: Talk to the children about the inflexibility (stiffness) of robots and the weightlessness of astronauts floating in outer space. Ask them to demonstrate first one and then the other. Repeat these alternating requests several times, always ending with the astronaut.

Curriculum Connections: *Science* is involved in exploring the contraction and release of muscles. Also, if you hold a discussion about the job of being an astronaut or the people who make robots, you'll bring in *social studies*.

I'm Melting

The process of melting fascinates children, and you can use this fascination to inspire relaxation.

To Have: No materials needed

To Do: Talk to the children about melting. Ask them to name some things that melt. Is it a fast process, or does it take place slowly?

Invite the children to demonstrate one or more of the following scenarios:

- ice cream on a hot day
- an ice cube left on the counter
- a snow person in the sun
- butter on a hot pancake
- a chocolate chip baking in a cookie

Curriculum Connections: Melting is a *science* concept, as is the relaxation of muscles.

Gentle Stretching

Stretching releases tension that has built up in the muscles. To really promote relaxation, encourage slow, gentle stretches.

To Have: A piece of quiet recorded music (optional)

To Do: Start the music (if you are using it). Then invite the children to stretch their bodies in upward, forward, and sideways directions. Next, ask them to gently stretch individual parts, like arms, legs, neck, and fingers. They can do this in standing or lying positions.

Curriculum Connections: Body-part identification falls under the content area of *science*. Include a discussion about muscles in the activity to fully make it a science experience.

Breath Rhythms

To Have: No materials needed

To Do: Instruct the children to make huge body shapes by starting small and then breathing in slowly, letting their bodies "grow" as they inhale. They then slowly exhale, curling themselves in toward the center of their bodies. Repeat this process until the children have grasped it, at which point you can ask them to do it even more slowly.

More to Do: A more challenging version of this activity is to ask the children to breathe in as though they are "growing" against some resistance and breathe out as though the resistance is gone.

Curriculum Connections: Asking the children to focus on their breath constitutes *science*. You can take it further by initiating a discussion about the lungs.

Point and Flex

To Have: No materials needed

To Do: Sit with the children and extend your legs in front of you, inviting the children to do the same. Demonstrate pointing your toes (pushing your toes away from your body and toward the floor) and flexing your toes (pulling your toes toward your body and the ceiling). Then chant the following poem, encouraging the children to follow its instructions (for the last line, the children will have to bend their knees and pull their feet closer to their bottoms):

> *Point the toes,*
> *Flex the toes,*
> *And point the toes once more.*
> *Now flex them up,*
> *Point them down,*
> *And rest them on the floor.*

Repeat this chant a couple of times. Then invite the children to shake out their legs and toes—or their whole body if they want.

More to Do: Ask the children if there are other body parts that can be pointed and flexed. The hands, arms, and neck are the most natural possibilities. Use the above chant, substituting a new body-part word for *toes*.

Curriculum Connections: The chant connects this activity to *emergent literacy*. To bring in *science*, discuss what's happening with the muscles as body parts are pointing and flexing.

Tight and Loose

To Have: No materials needed

To Do: Ask the children to make their bodies as tight as possible, bunching up their fists and hitching their shoulders up toward their ears. Count aloud from one to five, at which point you invite the children to make their bodies as loose as possible. Repeat this a few times.

Curriculum Connections: Counting is a simple *math* activity, while any consideration or discussion of what the muscles are doing brings in *science*.

Opening and Closing

To Have: No materials needed

To Do: Invite the children to get on the floor, curled up in the smallest shapes possible. As you count slowly to five, the children slowly open up their bodies until they're fully stretched out. You then count backward from five, during which time the children slowly return to their curled positions.

Once the children are comfortable with this activity, you can lengthen the count to ten, extending the time during which they're to curl and uncurl. This will require a lot more control.

Curriculum Connections: *Math* is included with the counting. Also, the self-regulation required brings in *social studies*.

Making Angels

To Have: No materials needed

To Do: Talk to the children about making angels in the snow. Have any of them ever done it? Then invite them to lie down on the floor, giving themselves enough room to stretch their arms and legs out to the side without touching anyone else. The children should begin with their legs straight and touching each other, with their arms by their sides. As you slowly count to ten, the children begin to open their legs wide and stretch their arms outward and upward, until they're stretched out as far as they can go. You then begin counting again, during which time the children begin to return their limbs to their original positions.

Curriculum Connections: *Math* is included with the counting. Also, the self-regulation required to move slowly brings in *social studies*.

Hug Yourself

The physical touch in this quick activity increases oxytocin, which is a feel-good hormone, and decreases cortisol, a stress hormone.

To Have: No materials needed

To Do: Invite the children to give themselves a nice, tight hug, holding for the count of ten. Repeat if necessary.

Curriculum Connections: The counting brings in simple *math*.

Cloud Watching

To Have: Clouds

To Do: Bring the children outdoors on a day when the sky is partly cloudy. Invite them to lie on their backs and look up at the clouds. Then ask them to tell you what shapes they see in the clouds. Are there animals? Vehicles? People?

Allow for some quiet time as well, during which the children can just engage with their imagination.

Curriculum Connections: Clouds are a component of weather and nature, falling under the content area of *science*.

A Listening Walk

There's a good deal of research demonstrating that nature has a calming effect on humans, so simply being outdoors is a good way to help children relax.

To Have: No materials needed

To Do: Take the children for a walk, encouraging them to listen for things in nature. For example, they might hear a dog barking, birds singing, or leaves rustling in the wind. When you return from the walk, ask the children to tell you about all the different things they heard.

Curriculum Connections: *Emergent literacy* is addressed through the active listening and discussion involved. And, of course, paying attention to nature makes this a *science* activity as well.

Discoveries in Nature

To Have: No materials needed

To Do: Bring the children outdoors and invite them to explore the area slowly and quietly, looking for something specific, such as an insect, a clover, a dandelion, or a pretty stone. When the designated item is found, the children should quietly observe it for a few moments. If it doesn't hold their attention for long, you can then assign them something else to discover.

Curriculum Connections: This is without a doubt a *science* experience, as nature, discovery, and observation all fall under that content area.

Listen to the Music

To Have: A piece of relaxing recorded music, plus mats (optional)

To Do: Simply invite the children to sit or lie comfortably, eyes closed, and listen to the music.

More to Do: Ask the children to listen for specific sounds in the music. If the piece has lyrics (which should be appropriate for relaxation), the children can listen for certain words. If it's instrumental, children might listen for when it gets slower or faster, or when the notes go higher or lower. Allow plenty of time for the children to absorb what they're hearing.

Curriculum Connections: This *music* appreciation activity also involves active listening, which is an element of *emergent literacy*.

Making Lemonade

To Have: Mats (optional)

To Do: Ask the children to sit on the floor or on mats, with their feet flat and their knees tucked to their chests. Now invite them to wrap their arms around their knees and squeeze as hard as they can, imagining their knees are lemons being juiced for lemonade. As the children are squeezing, slowly count to five. When you reach five, the children relax their hold, opening up their arms and legs and saying, "Ahhh." Repeat once or twice.

Curriculum Connections: The idea of making lemonade from lemons falls under nutrition, which is a component of *science*. The counting brings in a bit of *math*.

Imagine This

To Have: Mats (optional)

To Do: Invite the children to lie on their mats or on the floor. In a very quiet voice, ask them to imagine they are doing one of the first three choices below, and then end with the last option:

- floating on a cloud
- soaking in a warm tub
- drifting on a breeze
- drifting off to sleep

Curriculum Connections: Asking the children to use their imagination contributes to all content areas, but the cloud and the breeze are specifically about *science*. You might also initiate a discussion about what happens to the muscles when someone is soaking in a warm tub or drifting off to sleep. This brings in an additional aspect of science.

Imagining the Beach

To Have: Mats, if indoors (optional)

To Do: Ask the children to lie down and close their eyes. Paint a picture in their minds, inviting them to imagine they're at the beach. What sounds can they hear? The waves rolling in? Seagulls overhead? Can they feel the warm sun and the cool breeze and the soft blankets beneath them on the warm sand?

Curriculum Connections: All these images are part of nature, making the connection to *science*.

Listen Up

To Have: No materials needed

To Do: Explain to the children that you're going to set a timer for one minute and that during that time, you want them to sit quietly and simply listen. Invite them to close their eyes, and then start the timer. When the time is up, ask them to tell you some of the things they heard. (Quieting their minds may be difficult at first, but they'll get better at it with practice.)

Curriculum Connections: Both the active listening and speaking involved in this activity address *emergent literacy*.

Get Ready, Spaghetti

To Have: No materials needed

To Do: Divide the children into four groups. Ask each group to stand in one corner of the room.

Now invite the children to pretend they're pieces of uncooked spaghetti in a box. What would that look like? How would it feel? Would they be hard or soft? Straight or curving?

Next, ask the children to imagine there's a big pot of hot water in the center of the room. Invite them to make their way to the pot as though they are uncooked spaghetti.

Once they're in the pot, what happens? Invite the children to show you how they would look if they were cooked spaghetti!

Curriculum Connections: Discussing and exploring the contrast between uncooked and cooked spaghetti falls under the heading of nutrition, which belongs to the content area of *science*.

Being Healthy and Wise

To Have: No materials needed

To Do: To encourage the children to lie down and rest, you might want to discuss with them the concept that taking a nap or rest time each day is "healthy and wise." You might also want to address the idea of "letting muscles go." Then sing the following to the tune of "Itsy Bitsy Spider."

> *Let's lie down on our mats now,*
> *And rest our tired eyes.*
> *Taking a daily nap*
> *Is considered wise.*
> *So take this time to lie back,*
> *And let your muscles go.*
> *'Cause spending quiet time each day*
> *Is good for you, you know.*

Curriculum Connections: The song brings in *music*, while the lyrics contribute to *emergent literacy*.

Counting Sheep

To Have: No materials needed

To Do: Ask the children if they've ever heard the expression *counting sheep*. Explain that some people, when they have trouble falling asleep, close their eyes and imagine sheep jumping over a fence one at a time, and they count the sheep until they feel sleepy. Then sing the following song very slowly to the tune of "Bumping Up and Down in My Little Red Wagon." But first, invite the children to lie with their eyes closed, imagining the sheep.

One little,
Two little,
Three little sheep,
Four little,
Five little,
Six little sheep,
Seven little,
Eight little,
Nine little sheep,
Helping us to sleep!

Curriculum Connections: This activity offers children experience with counting (*math*) and with using their imagination. Also, the song brings in *music*, while the lyrics and active listening address *emergent literacy*.

A Bit of Brahms

To Have: No materials needed

To Do: This song, sung to the tune of "Brahms's Lullaby," is most effective if you can sing to the children individually by name, tiptoeing from mat to mat:

Rest your eyes,
Rest your eyes.
Rest your eyes, little _____.
Let your body relax.
Feel the peace that it brings.

Curriculum Connections: *Music* and *emergent literacy* are addressed here, with the song and lyrics.

Breathing Buddies

To Have: One stuffed animal per child (brought from home if necessary)

To Do: Invite the children to lie on their backs and to place their stuffed animals on their tummies. They then watch the animals move up and down as they gently and slowly breathe in and out.

Curriculum Connections: Awareness of the breath constitutes *science*, as does any discussion of the lungs' functions.

Breathing Buddies II

To Have: No materials needed

To Do: The children pair off and sit back-to-back on the floor. Ask the children to pay attention to the breathing of their partner. Is it slow and deep? Can they feel the movement of their partner's back as the person breathes in and out?

Curriculum Connections: Because this is a cooperative activity, it falls under the heading of *social studies*. *Science* is also addressed through awareness of breathing and any discussion of the lungs.

Feeling Calm, Feeling Nervous

To Have: No materials needed

To Do: Talk to the children about the fact that feeling calm is feeling very relaxed, like the feeling experienced just before falling asleep at night. At those times, muscles feel loose and "liquid." Feeling nervous, on the other hand, is a combination of feeling scared and feeling worried.

Ask the children to tell you about times they've felt calm and times they've felt nervous. Invite them to show you the difference with their bodies.

With the children standing, explain that when you say, "Calm," they should make their bodies as relaxed as possible. When you say, "Nervous," they should tense up. Vary the amount of time between verbal cues, and use your voice to convey the meaning of the word you're saying. Repeat this process several times, always ending with the word *calm*.

More to Do: You can repeat this process with the children kneeling, sitting, and lying down.

Curriculum Connections: A discussion about the amount of muscle tension people experience when they are calm or nervous brings in the content area of *science*. A discussion of the opposites involved here creates an experience in *emergent literacy*.

A Sleeping Contest

If you have a particularly competitive group of children, you might want to try this contest. But remember, there is never really a winner. You should validate the sleeping abilities of the entire group.

To Have: Mats or cots (optional)

To Do: Once the children are lying down, invite them to show you who can sleep the soundest—without snoring. (If you don't add that caveat, you're likely to end up with the walls vibrating!) Once the children are all demonstrating the appropriate response, tell them, in your quietest naptime or rest time voice, that they are the best sleeping class you've ever seen.

Curriculum Connections: A discussion about sleep brings in the content area of *science*.

"It's Time to Rest Now"

To Have: No materials needed

To Do: Sing the following song to the children (either to the group as a whole or to children individually) who might be having trouble relaxing. Sing it to the tune of "You Are My Sunshine":

> *It's time to rest now,*
> *And have some quiet.*
> *To be silent for a while.*
> *And once we're rested,*
> *We will feel better,*
> *And we'll get up with a smile.*

Curriculum Connections: The song and lyrics make this an experience in both *music* and *emergent literacy*.

Low Batteries

To Have: No materials needed

To Do: Talk to the children about battery-operated objects like toothbrushes or toy vehicles. What happens when the batteries begin to die? Ask the children to first act out their chosen battery-operated object while the battery is strong and then show you its gradual slowdown. Finally, they should demonstrate a full stop.

Curriculum Connections: The topic of battery-powered objects fits under *science*.

Being Bears

To Have: No materials needed

To Do: Talk to the children about bears hibernating in the winter. Then ask them to show you how a bear would lumber off to its cave and fall asleep for the winter.

Curriculum Connections: The concept of animals hibernating falls under the content area of *science*.

Conclusion

As you lead the children through the experiences in this book, I am confident that you will become a believer in the mind-body connection, in the importance of engaging multiple senses, and in the value of active learning. You will discover that the children are better able to focus and are more engaged throughout the day. That focus and engagement will translate into enhanced learning—and yes, standards met. Because the results will speak for themselves, you will have less need to justify using active learning in your setting. Parents and administrators will become believers too.

Of course, it's likely that you purchased this book because you want to avoid behavior challenges. I am convinced that the approaches and activities in *Acting Out!* will not only promote improved learning experiences but will also help foster a more positive environment.

Today's children are frustrated because they are given fewer and fewer opportunities to play and because they are being asked to accomplish tasks for which they are not yet developmentally equipped. As they are unable to meet the demands of the important adults in their lives, their frustration grows. Many children act out in response to that frustration. Their inability to express themselves verbally means that misbehavior is the only way they can express their dismay.

As you respect the stages of child development and children's natural ways of learning, the children in your setting will be happier and calmer, and they will respect you in return. The focus on cooperative and circle games will help ensure that the children respect one another as well—both their similarities and their differences. These are the secrets that will help you avoid behavior challenges.

Index of Activities by Title

References

Adams, Susan. 2013. "The 10 Skills Employers Most Want in 20-Something Employees." *Forbes*, October 11. www.forbes.com/sites/susanadams/2013/10/11/the-10-skills-employers-most -want-in-20-something-employees/#4027b87b6330.

Bitsko, Rebecca H., Joseph R. Holbrook, Rheem M. Ghandour, Stephen J. Blumberg, Susanna N. Visser, Ruth Perou, and John T. Walkup. 2018. "Epidemiology and Impact of Health Care Provider–Diagnosed Anxiety and Depression among US Children." *Journal of Developmental and Behavioral Pediatrics* 39, no. 5 (June): 395–403.

Breus, Michael J. 2017. "5 Relaxation Techniques for Better Sleep." *Psychology Today*, January 1. www.psychologytoday.com/us/blog/sleep-newzzz/201701/5-relaxation-techniques-better -sleep.

Bright, Rebecca. 2018. "Kids Who Can't Sit Still." National Education Association. Accessed December 12. www.nea.org/tools/47003.htm.

Butler, Shelley. 2005. "Circle Time Is the Right Time." *Earlychildhood NEWS* 17 (1): 28–30. www .earlychildhoodnews.com/earlychildhood/article_view.aspx?ArticleID=537.

Cherry, Clare. 1971. *Creative Movement for the Developing Child: A Nursery School Handbook for Non-Musicians.* Belmont, CA: Fearon.

———. 1981. *Think of Something Quiet: A Guide for Achieving Serenity in Early Childhood Classrooms.* Belmont, CA: Pitman Learning.

Corso, Marjorie. 1993. "Is Developmentally Appropriate Physical Education the Answer to Children's School Readiness?" *Colorado Journal of Health, Physical Education, Recreation, and Dance* 19 (2): 6–7.

Crain, William. 2001. "How Nature Helps Children." *Montessori Life* 13, no. 3 (Summer): 22–24.

Dornhecker, Marianela, Jamilia Blake, Mark Benden, Hongwei Zhao, and Monica Wendel. 2015. "The Effect of Stand-Biased Desks on Academic Engagement: An Exploratory Study." *International Journal of Health Promotion and Education* 53 (5): 271–80.

Godwin, Karrie E., Ma Victoria Almeda, Howard Seltman, Shi Min Kai, Mandi D. Skerbetz, Ryan S. Baker, and Anna V. Fisher. 2016. "Off-Task Behavior in Elementary School Children." *Learning and Instruction* 44 (August): 128–43.

Hanish, Laura D., and Richard A. Fabes. 2014. "Peer Socialization of Gender in Young Boys and Girls." Encyclopedia on Early Childhood Development. www.child-encyclopedia.com /gender-early-socialization/according-experts/peer-socialization-gender-young-boys-and -girls.

Hannaford, Carla. 2007. *Smart Moves: Why Learning Is Not All in Your Head.* Salt Lake City, UT: Great River Books.

Hanscom, Angela. 2014. "The Real Reason Why Kids Fidget." *Huffington Post*, Last modified December 6, 2017. www.huffingtonpost.com/angela-hanscom/the-real-reason-why-kids -fidget_b_5586265.html.

Immordino-Yang, Mary Helen. 2016. *Emotions, Learning, and the Brain: Exploring the Educational Implications of Affective Neuroscience.* New York: W. W. Norton and Company.

IPA/USA (International Play Association USA Affiliate). 2019. "Promoting Recess." Accessed January 31. www.ipausa.org/recess_pages/promoting_recess.html.

Jaques-Dalcroze, Émile. 1931. *Eurhythmics, Art, and Education.* Translated by Frederick Rothwell. New York: Barnes.

Jarrett, Olga S., and Darlene M. Maxwell. 2000. "What Research Says about the Need for Recess." In *Elementary School Recess: Selected Readings, Games, and Activities for Teachers and Parents*, edited by Rhonda L. Clements, 12–23. Lake Charles, LA: American Press.

Jensen, Eric. 2000. *Learning with the Body in Mind: The Scientific Basis for Energizers, Movement, Play, Games, and Physical Education*. San Diego, CA: Brain Store.

Kamenetz, Anya. 2015. "Vindication for Fidgeters: Movement May Help Students with ADHD Concentrate." National Public Radio, May 14. www.npr.org/sections/ed/2015/05/14 /404959284/fidgeting-may-help-concentration-for-students-with-adhd.

Kohl, Harold W., III, and Heather D. Cook, eds. 2013. *Educating the Student Body: Taking Physical Activity and Physical Education to School*. Washington, DC: National Academies Press.

Kohn, Alfie. 1992. *No Contest: The Case against Competition*. Rev. ed. Boston: Houghton Mifflin.

Kristof, Nicholas D. 1998. "Correspondence/Uncompetitive in Tokyo; In Japan, Nice Guys (and Girls) Finish Together." *New York Times*, April 12.

Malone, Karen, and Paul Tranter. 2003. "Children's Environmental Learning and the Use, Design and Management of Schoolgrounds." *Children, Youth and Environments* 13 (2): 87–137.

Martin, David Jerner, and Kimberly S. Loomis. 2007. *Building Teachers: A Constructivist Approach to Introducing Education*. Belmont, CA: Wadsworth.

Miller, Darla Ferris. 2016. *Positive Child Guidance*. 8th ed. Boston, MA: Cengage Learning.

Moore, Robin. 1996. "Compact Nature: The Role of Playing and Learning Gardens in Children's Lives." *Journal of Therapeutic Horticulture* 8:72–82.

Orlick, Terry. 1982. *The Second Cooperative Sports and Games Book*. New York: Pantheon.

———. 2006. *Cooperative Games and Sports: Joyful Activities for Everyone*. Champaign, IL: Human Kinetics.

Pica, Rae. 2019a. "Creating Praise Junkies: Are You Giving Children Too Much 'Positive Reinforcement'?" Interview with Ellen Ava Sigler, Margaret Berry Wilson, and Deborah J. Stewart. BAM Radio broadcast, 10:35. Accessed January 28. www.bamradionetwork.com /educators-channel/618-creating-praise-junkies-are-you-giving-children-too-much -positive-reinforcement.

Pica, Rae. 2019b. "Developing Genuine versus Phony Self-Esteem in Children." Interview with Stanley Greenspan. BAM Radio broadcast, 8:14. Accessed January 28. www.bamradionetwork .com/educators-channel/155-developing-genuine-versus-phony-self-esteem-in-children.

Pica, Rae. 2019c. "Have Children Lost Their Ability to Play?" Interview with Nancy Carlsson-Paige. BAM Radio broadcast, 12:48. Accessed January 28. www.bamradionetwork.com/student -centric-strategies/4553-have-children-lost-their-ability-to-play.

Pica, Rae. 2019d. "Spatial Skills and STEM: What's the Connection?" Interview with Kathy Hirsh-Pasek, Roberta Michnick Golinkoff, and Jill Berkowicz. BAM Radio broadcast, 8:44. Accessed January 28. www.bamradionetwork.com/student-centric-strategies/4295 -understanding-spacial-skills-and-stem-in-early-education.

Pica, Rae. 2019e. "Teaching Strategies: Handling Young Students Who Just Won't Sit Still." Interview with Christy Isbell, Holly Robinson, Carla Hannaford, and Susan Latanzi Roser. BAM Radio broadcast, 10:35. Accessed January 28. www.bamradionetwork.com/educators -channel/326-teaching-strategieshandling-young-students-who-just-wont-sit-still.

Ratey, John J. 2008. *Spark: The Revolutionary New Science of Exercise and the Brain*. New York: Little, Brown.

Sarver, Dustin E., Mark D. Rapport, Michael J. Kofler, Joseph S. Raiker, and Lauren M. Friedman. 2015. "Hyperactivity in Attention Deficit/Hyperactivity Disorder (ADHD): Impairing Deficit or Compensatory Behavior?" *Journal of Abnormal Child Psychology* 43, no. 7 (October): 1219–32. http://doi.org/10.1007/s10802-015-0011-1.

Skibbe, Lori E., Janelle J. Montroy, Ryan P. Bowles, and Frederick J. Morrison. 2019. "Self-Regulation and the Development of Literacy and Language Achievement from Preschool through Second Grade." *Early Childhood Research Quarterly* 46 (First Quarter): 240–51. http://doi.org/10.1016/j.ecresq.2018.02.005.

Sobko, Tanja, Zhenzhen Jia, and Gavin Brown. 2018. "Measuring Connectedness to Nature in Preschool Children in an Urban Setting and Its Relation to Psychological Functioning." *PLoS ONE* 13 (11): e0207057. http://doi.org/10.1371/journal.pone.0207057.

Summerford, Cathie. 2009. *Action-Packed Classrooms, K–5: Using Movement to Educate and Invigorate Learners.* Thousand Oaks, CA: Corwin.

Taylor, Andrea Faber, Frances E. Kuo, and William C. Sullivan. 2001. "Coping with ADD: The Surprising Connection to Green Play Settings." *Environment and Behavior* 33 (1): 54–77.

Trambley, Elisabeth. 2017. "Breaks in the Elementary Classroom and Their Effect on Student Behavior." Master's thesis, California State University, Monterey Bay. digitalcommons.csumb.edu/cgi/viewcontent.cgi?article=1133&context=caps_thes_all.

Vogel, Susanne, and Lars Schwabe. 2016. "Learning and Memory under Stress: Implications for the Classroom." *NPJ Science of Learning* 1: 16011. http://doi.org/10.1038/npjscilearn.2016.11.

Walker, Timothy D. 2017. *Teach Like Finland: 33 Simple Strategies for Joyful Classrooms.* New York: W. W. Norton and Company.

Wells, Nancy M. 2000. "At Home with Nature: Effects of 'Greenness' on Children's Cognitive Functioning." *Environment and Behavior* 32 (6): 775–95.

Whitehead, Alfred North. 1967. *The Aims of Education and Other Essays.* New York: Free Press.

Willis, Judy. 2016. "Memorizing: Faster, Easier, Longer Lasting, and More Fun." *Psychology Today*, September 5. www.psychologytoday.com/us/blog/radical-teaching/201609/memorizing-faster-easier-longer-lasting-and-more-fun.